Other Publications:

THE GOOD COOK
THE SEAFARERS
THE ENCYCLOPEDIA OF COLLECTIBLES
THE GREAT CITIES
WORLD WAR II
THE WORLD'S WILD PLACES
THE TIME-LIFE LIBRARY OF BOATING
HUMAN BEHAVIOR
THE ART OF SEWING
THE OLD WEST
THE EMERGENCE OF MAN
THE AMERICAN WILDERNESS
THE TIME-LIFE ENCYCLOPEDIA OF GARDENING
LIFE LIBRARY OF PHOTOGRAPHY
THIS FABULOUS CENTURY
FOODS OF THE WORLD
TIME-LIFE LIBRARY OF AMERICA
TIME-LIFE LIBRARY OF ART
GREAT AGES OF MAN
LIFE SCIENCE LIBRARY
THE LIFE HISTORY OF THE UNITED STATES
TIME READING PROGRAM
LIFE NATURE LIBRARY
LIFE WORLD LIBRARY
FAMILY LIBRARY:
    HOW THINGS WORK IN YOUR HOME
    THE TIME-LIFE BOOK OF THE FAMILY CAR
    THE TIME-LIFE FAMILY LEGAL GUIDE
    THE TIME-LIFE BOOK OF FAMILY FINANCE

HOME REPAIR
AND IMPROVEMENT

BUILT-INS

BY THE EDITORS OF
TIME-LIFE BOOKS

TIME-LIFE BOOKS
ALEXANDRIA, VIRGINIA

Time-Life Books Inc.
is a wholly owned subsidiary of
TIME INCORPORATED

Founder Henry R. Luce 1898-1967

Editor-in-Chief Henry Anatole Grunwald
Chairman of the Board Andrew Heiskell
President James R. Shepley
Editorial Director Ralph Graves
Vice Chairman Arthur Temple

TIME-LIFE BOOKS INC.

Managing Editor Jerry Korn
Executive Editor David Maness
Assistant Managing Editors Dale M. Brown (planning), George Constable,
George G. Daniels (acting), Martin Mann,
John Paul Porter
Art Director Tom Suzuki
Chief of Research David L. Harrison
Director of Photography Robert G. Mason
Senior Text Editor Diana Hirsh
Assistant Art Director Arnold C. Holeywell
Assistant Chief of Research Carolyn L. Sackett
Assistant Director of Photography Dolores A. Littles

Chairman Joan D. Manley
President John D. McSweeney
Executive Vice Presidents Carl G. Jaeger, John Steven Maxwell, David J. Walsh
Vice Presidents Nicholas Benton (public relations), John L. Canova
(sales), Nicholas J. C. Ingleton (Asia), James L. Mercer
(Europe/South Pacific), Herbert Sorkin (production),
Paul R. Stewart (promotion), Peter G. Barnes
Personnel Director Beatrice T. Dobie
Consumer Affairs Director Carol Flaumenhaft
Comptroller George Artandi

HOME REPAIR AND IMPROVEMENT

Editorial Staff for Built-ins

Editor William Frankel
Assistant Editor David Thiemann
Designer Kenneth E. Hancock
Picture Editor Adrian Allen
Associate Designer Lorraine D. Rivard
Text Editors Bonnie Bohling Kreitler, Leslie Marshall, Lydia Preston,
Brooke Stoddard
Staff Writers Lynn R. Addison, William C. Banks, Megan Barnett,
Robert A. Doyle, Malachy Duffy, Steven J. Forbis,
Peter Pocock, William Worsley
Chief Researcher Phyllis K. Wise
Art Associates George Bell, Daniel J. McSweeney, Richard Whiting
Editorial Assistant Susanne S. Trice

Editorial Production

Production Editor Douglas B. Graham
Operations Manager Gennaro C. Esposito, Gordon E. Buck (assistant)
Assistant Production Editor Feliciano Madrid
Quality Control Robert L. Young (director), James J. Cox (assistant),
Michael G. Wight (associate)
Art Coordinator Anne B. Landry
Copy Staff Susan B. Galloway (chief), Margery duMond,
Cynthia Kleinfeld, Brian Miller, Celia Beattie
Picture Department Renée DeSandies
Traffic Jeanne Potter

Correspondents: Elisabeth Kraemer (Bonn); Margot
Hapgood, Dorothy Bacon, Lesley Coleman (London);
Susan Jonas, Lucy T. Voulgaris (New York); Maria
Vincenza Aloisi, Josephine du Brusle (Paris); Ann
Natanson (Rome). Valuable assistance was also
provided by: **Carolyn** T. Chubet, Miriam Hsia (New
York); Mimi Murphy (Rome).

THE CONSULTANTS: After studying architecture at
the Boston Architectural Center, Lawrence R. England Jr. began his association with L. R. England and
Sons, a family custom cabinetmaking and woodcarving business started by his grandfather in 1900.

Robert L. Petersen has been a cabinetmaker in Maryland and Virginia since 1971. His own specialty is 18th
Century Palladian design and architecture.

Yves A. Fedrigault began working as a cabinetmaker
at the age of 16 in Bordeaux, France. He moved to the
United States in 1963, and in 1965 he started his own
business, Y. A. F. Development, Inc., which specializes
in custom-made built-ins and in the restoration and
remodeling of old houses.

Roswell W. Ard is a consulting structural engineer
and a professional home inspector in northern Michigan. He has written professional papers on woodframe construction techniques.

Harris Mitchell, a special consultant for Canada, has
worked in the field of home repair and improvement
for more than two decades. He is editor of the magazine Canadian Homes and author of a syndicated
newspaper column, "You Wanted to Know," as well
as a number of books on home improvement.

For information about any Time-Life book, please write:
Reader Information
Time-Life Books
541 North Fairbanks Court
Chicago, Illinois 60611

Library of Congress Cataloging in Publication Data
Time-Life Books.
    Built-ins.
    (Home repair and improvement)
    Includes index.
    1. Built-in furniture.   I. Title.
TT197.5.B8T55   1979   684.1'6   79-18674
ISBN 0-8094-2432-0
ISBN 0-8094-2431-2 lib. bdg.

Contents

1

Cabinets Plain and Fancy

To most people, the word "built-in" stands for two standard elements of a modern house—kitchen cabinets and living-room bookcases. In fact, the convenience of built-ins has spread throughout the house, in room dividers, buffets, storage walls and appliance covers; in benches, couches and tables; and in beds that fold into the walls. Some built-ins even create whole new living areas—raised dining platforms, sunken conversation pits and overhead lofts.

Whatever the location or use, a built-in is inexpensive, often costing hundreds of dollars less than its factory-made equivalent. It fits a particular room and particular needs, without wasted space or an awkward arrangement of doors or drawers. And its workmanship is suited to its surroundings—a backless bookcase for a child's bedroom, perhaps, a fine hardwood cabinet for a dining room.

Solid lumber can serve for simple built-ins such as shelves, open bookcases *(opposite)* and small drawers; it is easy to cut and finish, and inexpensive woods such as pine come in widths as great as 11¼ inches. However, fine woods are prohibitively expensive in pieces even that wide, and most built-ins require wood wider yet. As a result the common material for built-ins is plywood.

To a woodworker, plywood has great advantages. It comes in unblemished sheets with straight edges and a uniform thickness, and each part of a built-in can be made from a single section. It does not warp or twist, and seldom splits or cracks. Perhaps more important, it is inexpensive—roughly half the price of board lumber.

So-called hardwood plywood, the type most commonly used for built-ins, has hardwood face veneers and inner plies of less expensive softwood. Birch is best for surfaces to be painted or stained. Birch grain is not particularly attractive, however; if a clear finish is to be applied, more expensive woods, such as cherry and oak, are generally preferred. For maximum economy, softwood plywood, which has face veneers of pine or fir, is often employed; its garish grain makes it difficult to finish attractively.

Each face of a hardwood plywood sheet is graded: A (or Premium) grade has unblemished faces, which are matched for color and grain; the more common 1 (or Good) grade, less evenly matched, is generally used with stains or clear finishes; 2 (or Sound) grade has minor imperfections and is used to construct cabinets that will be painted; 3 (or Utility) grade, used for hidden cabinet parts, has splits and open knotholes. A sheet labeled 1-3 would have one good side and one that has splits and knotholes, and should be used where only the good side will be visible. If you use softwood plywood, grade A-A, which has two unblemished faces, and grade A-C, which has one good face and one bad one, are recommended.

Open Shelving: An Assembly Built onto a Wall

The simplest of all built-ins is a set of open shelves nailed to the walls piece by piece. Made with plain butt joints, such shelving is easier to install than a cabinet made in a workshop *(pages 16-19)* because it need not be maneuvered on stairs or through doorways, or painstakingly shaped to the contours of the walls. Yet properly built, it attractively fills a variety of uses, from turning an ordinary closet into a linen closet to creating an informal bookcase.

Most open shelves are rectangular, and fit into the corner of a room or a three-sided enclosure of walls—in a closet, for example, or between a fireplace and a corner. Some are triangular to take advantage of a corner, generally for storage or display (a wooden triangle makes a poor bookshelf). Shelves of either type can be supported by a simple system of adjustable clips that snap into vertical metal standards. In open shelving the standards generally are surface-mounted, creating a gap of about 3/16 inch at the ends of each shelf; for a neater finish, the standards can be set into a vertical dado, or groove *(page 22)*.

The dimensions of shelving units depend on the room and the purpose. In height they should leave at least 1 foot of workspace between the top and the ceiling; after the top is nailed down, the gap can be covered with a soffit *(page 51)*. The length of the unit can be anything you like. The length of a single shelf should not exceed 32 inches, although some commercial units extend to 36 inches; in longer units, use partitions to support shelves of 32 inches or less. The depth of the shelves depends on what you plan to store on them. Paperback books and most hardbacks will fit on shelves 8 inches deep; large books, such as encyclopedias and art books, need 10- to 12-inch shelves; records require 13 inches, stereo equipment 18 or more, and a TV at least 24.

Shelves up to 11¼ inches deep can be made from ordinary 1-inch lumber. For deeper shelves, use ¾-inch grade AX-A plywood; the exposed plywood edges can be concealed with veneer tape or covered with wood filler and painted or, best of all, covered with ⅛-inch wooden edge bands. A table saw provides maximum speed and precision *(pages 13-15)*, although simpler tools may suffice.

Before beginning construction, try to pry the baseboard from the walls that will contain the shelving. Starting at a corner, lever the baseboard out with a pry bar, using a wooden block as a fulcrum to protect the wall; slip a wooden wedge behind the baseboard to hold it away from the wall, then move the pry bar about 16 inches at a time. (You can cut and reuse the old baseboard to trim any wall space left on each side of the shelving.) If the baseboard is pinned behind layers of flooring, leave it in place but scribe and cut the base of the shelving to its shape *(page 48)*.

If you have taken the baseboard off, you will find clues to the locations of the studs behind the wall: the bottoms of wallboard-tape seams that lie over studs, or the nail holes where the baseboard was secured. To confirm these locations, tap lightly on the wall until you hear the solid sound that usually comes from a stud; if necessary, drill ⅛-inch holes and probe inside the wall with a length of wire until you hit the studs.

Rectangular Shelves along a Wall

1 **Making the base.** For shelves in a corner, assemble the base first using 1-inch lumber cut to the height of the room baseboard. The long pieces should be ¾ inch shorter than the length of the shelving unit; make the short end pieces 4½ inches shorter than the depth of the unit. Set the pieces on edge in a rectangle and nail through each long piece into the ends of the short ones with three sixpenny finishing nails; angle the nails slightly toward the inside of the rectangle. Set the base into the corner and nail the back and the sidepieces to each wall stud with two eightpenny nails; where you cannot nail into studs, use hollow-wall anchors.

To build shelves into a recess *(inset)*, cut front and back pieces to the length of the back of the recess and nail the back piece to studs in the wall; nail the sidepieces to the flanking walls, then fasten the front piece to the sides.

2 **The bottom shelf and sides.** For these and other parts, use 1-inch lumber or, if shelves are deeper than 11¼ inches, ¾-inch plywood. Nail to the base a bottom shelf as long as the base and 3 inches wider, driving sixpenny finishing nails every 6 inches. Fasten to the corner wall a side as wide as the bottom shelf and long enough to reach from the shelf to the underside of the unit top, using finishing nails or wall anchors.

For a corner unit, cut the other sidepiece to reach from the floor to the underside of the unit's top and make a notch in the lower front corner 3 inches wide and the height of the base.

For a recessed unit, cut a second sidepiece to match the first and fasten it to the wall at the other side of the wall recess.

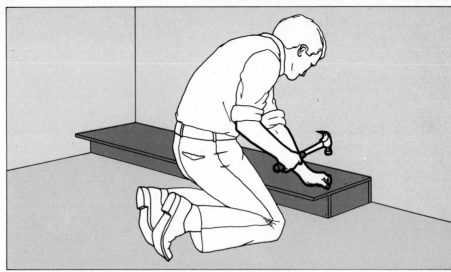

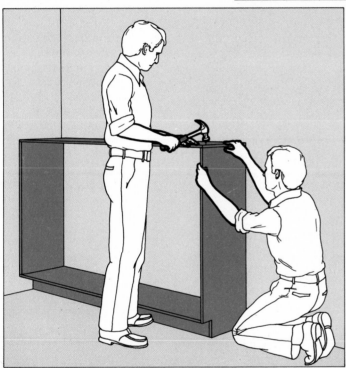

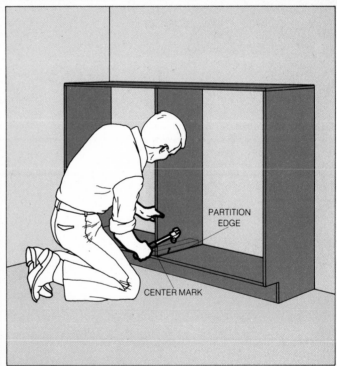

3 **Nailing the top.** For a corner unit, cut a top that is ¾ inch longer than the bottom shelf. Place the top on the sides—have a helper hold the loose sidepiece in place—set a piece of cardboard against the corner wall to protect it from the hammer, and butt-nail the top to each side with sixpenny finishing nails every 6 inches. Fasten the bottom of the exposed sidepiece to the base with sixpenny nails every 4 inches.

For a unit built in a recess, measure between the top outer edges of the sidepieces at the front and at the back, cut the top to these dimensions and butt-nail it to the sides.

4 **Installing the partitions.** Toenail partitions, the same size as the corner sidepiece, to divide the unit into sections no wider than 32 inches. To make equal spaces, divide the inside length of the unit by the number of spaces, and mark off, on top and bottom, spaces of this size measured from a side. Then, ⅜ inch to one side of each mark, draw a line for the partition edge, using a combination square.

Face-nail the partition through the top of the unit with sixpenny nails every 6 inches. Nail a scrap of wood along the line on the bottom (inset), tap the partition tight against the scrap and toenail sixpenny nails every 8 inches through the partition into the bottom; remove the scrap and toenail the partition from the other side.

5 **Installing the standards.** Near the top and bottom of each side, mark the wood 1 inch from the front and from the back. On each partition, mark one side 1 inch from the back and 1½ inches from the front, the other side 1½ inches from the back and 1 inch from the front. Set a standard just inside each top-and-bottom pair of marks, with its lower end resting directly on the bottom shelf of the unit; drill pilot holes through the screw holes in the standard and fasten the standard with the screws provided by the manufacturer. Snap shelf clips (inset) into the standards at the levels of the shelves.

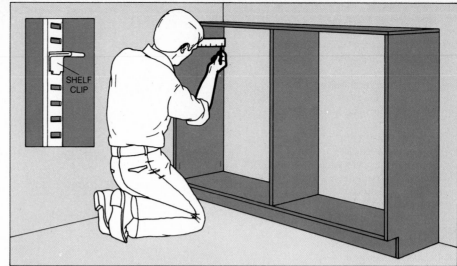

6 **Cutting the shelves.** On the bottom shelf of the unit and at each set of shelf clips, measure between the standards at the front and back of the cabinet. Cut a shelf that is ⅛ inch shorter than the shortest of the measurements you took, and set it on the clips.

Triangular Shelves for a Corner

1 **Making a template.** Cut a piece of ¾-inch plywood into a square with sides about 2 inches longer than the planned sides of the shelves and, measuring from a corner, mark the length of the shelf sides—usually about 18 inches—on two edges of the plywood square. Using a straightedge, draw a line between the marks for the front of the cabinet, and a parallel line 3 inches closer to the corner for the front of the base. To check the layout, use a combination square to draw a 45° line from the corner to the cabinet-front line (inset); this line should be exactly half as long as the front line.

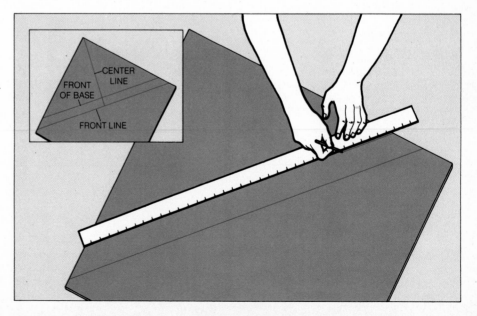

2 **Making the base.** To mark the front of the base, select a 1-inch board as wide as the baseboard of the room and set it on edge, just behind the line for the front of the base. Trace a short line on the template along the back of the board at each edge of the template. Mark the position of each edge of the template on the front and back of the board *(top)*. At each pair of marks, cut the board at a 45° angle.

To mark the sides of the base, set a 1-inch board on the edge of the template, with the end of the board at the template's corner. Mark the front and back of this board where it touches the traced lines; set a second 1-inch board on the other side of the template, butted against the first *(bottom)*, and mark it in the same way. Cut the sides to 45° angles at the marks and fasten them to the walls; nail the frontpiece to the ends of the sidepieces *(page 8, Step 1)*.

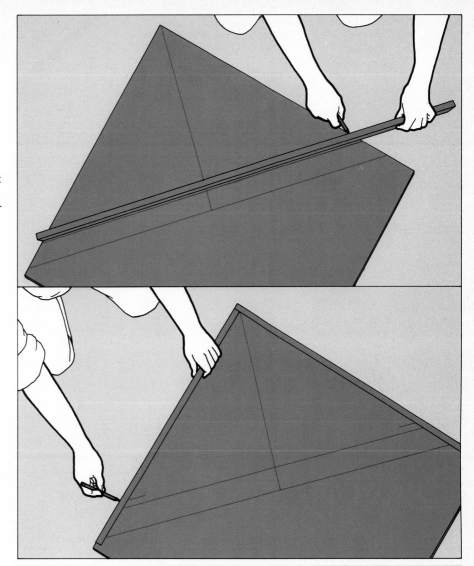

3 **Cutting the bottom of the unit.** Cut the template along the line for the front of the unit. If you use a portable circular saw, measure the distance between the side of the blade and the left edge of the base plate, temporarily nail a straightedge this distance from the marked line and run the base plate along the straightedge to make the cut. Fasten the bottom to the base with sixpenny finishing nails every 6 inches.

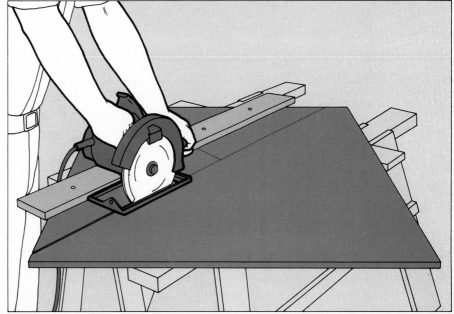

4 Beveling the sides. On the bottom shelf, measure the distance from the corner of the wall to the 45° corner of the triangle; mark this across the face of a sidepiece. Using a circular or table saw, cut the piece lengthwise with a 45° bevel cut that matches the angle of the base, then cut the piece to the desired height and fasten it to the wall *(page 9, Step 3)*. Fit the second sidepiece by butting it against the first at the corner, and cut it in the same way.

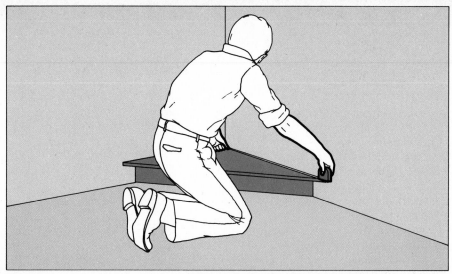

5 Marking the top. Set the other half of the template atop the sidepieces, with the square corner snug against the corner of the wall, and mark the outer corners of the sidepieces on the underside of the template. Cut the top as you did the bottom *(above)* and nail it to the sides.

Install shelf standards on each sidepiece, 1 inch from the front edge and 2 inches from the back, and snap in the shelf clips *(page 10, Step 5)*. To mark and cut the shelves, set rectangular pieces of plywood on the clips, mark them at the corners of the sidepieces and cut them along a line drawn ¼ inch inside the marks.

6 Finishing the edges. Cover the exposed plywood edges of the unit with ⅜-inch edge bands, mitered to match the angles of the shelving. Squeeze a bead of white glue along each edge and smear it along the edge evenly with your finger. Press the edge band into the glue, flush with the edges of the plywood; wherever you squeeze wet glue out of a joint, wipe it off immediately—do not let it dry. When the glued joints have dried—generally after an hour or so—fasten the bands with 1-inch brads every 6 inches.

A Table Saw for Precise Cuts and Joints

A portable circular saw with jigs and guides *(page 11)* is adequate for almost any built-in, but the tool preferred by professionals is the table saw. The blade of a table saw protrudes through a slot in a perfectly flat metal table. For cuts with the grain, an adjustable rip fence clamps onto the table, parallel to the blade; for crosscuts and angle cuts, an adjustable miter gauge is used.

A 10-inch table saw—the size most common in home workshops—has a blade 10 inches in diameter and will cut through a board 3¼ inches thick. The rip capacity, measured between the rip fence and the side of the blade, ideally should be at least 24 inches, so that the saw can cut along the center of a 4-by-8 sheet of plywood; on some models this cut may require an outrigger table. In addition, there should be at least 12 inches between the front of the table and the edge of the blade, to accommodate a 1-by-12 board for a crosscut.

A hollow-ground combination blade (sometimes called a planer blade) can make both rip cuts and crosscuts; as a second blade, you may want a fine-toothed crosscut blade, which reduces chipping and splintering. These blades, made of ordinary steel, require frequent professional sharpening; if you do a great deal of sawing, you may want to invest in a more durable—and expensive—carbide-tipped blade with about 40 teeth.

The blade of a table saw rotates toward the operator. To reduce the risk of injury, the blade is covered with a plastic guard, and two devices—a plate called a splitter and a set of antikickback fingers *(right)*—prevent a board from binding or kicking back. If kickbacks do occur, make sure the blade is still sharp, then check and adjust the alignment of the saw according to the manufacturer's instructions. To prevent splintering of surfaces that will show in the completed job, always saw boards with the hidden side down—the bottom surface chips more than the top—and feed boards into the blade slowly, for a fast feed makes rough cuts and increases the risk of kickback.

Anatomy of a table saw. The blade of this saw protrudes through a slot in the tabletop and is covered by a pivoting plastic guard that slides over a board as it is cut. Inside the guard, a splitter behind the blade keeps the saw kerf from binding on the blade, and spring-loaded antikickback fingers dig into a board if the blade begins to kick it back. The blade height is adjusted by a crank beneath the table; the blade tilt, by a knurled handwheel behind the crank.

The miter gauge, used to guide crosscuts and angle cuts, ordinarily slides in the groove at the left side of the blade, but can also be used in a right-hand groove. The gauge has stops at 90° and 45°, and can be locked at other angles with a knob. A homemade wooden extension is screwed to the face of the gauge to keep long boards from wobbling as they are cut. The rip fence slides on guide bars at the front and back of the table and can be locked at any position on the bars. For narrow rip cuts, a wooden face is fastened to the inside of the fence to protect the saw blade; this face also is used to prevent panels less than ¼ inch thick from slipping underneath the regular fence. For rip or dado cuts made on the edges or ends of boards, a tall wooden face is used for extra support.

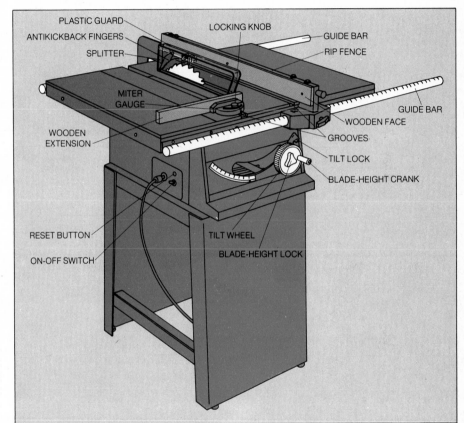

Safety Tips for Table Saws

In addition to the common-sense rules that apply to the use of all power tools—wear goggles and comfortable but not loose clothes—special precautions are required for a table saw:
- ☐ Adjust the saw before you turn it on, never while it is running.
- ☐ Before cutting knotty boards, knock large or loose knots out with a hammer.
- ☐ Never saw boards freehand; always use a rip fence or a miter gauge.
- ☐ If the blade stalls, turn the saw off immediately; do not try to free a stalled blade while the motor is on.
- ☐ Do not touch waste pieces less than a foot long before the blade stops.
- ☐ Never reach over or behind the blade—a kickback could yank your hand into the blade.
- ☐ Always keep your hands far away from the blade, using a push stick as needed to guide the work.

Setting Up for the Basic Cuts

Crosscutting. Set the miter gauge at 90°, place the edge of the board against the gauge and set the blade so its top is about ⅛ inch above the board. Align the marked cutting line with the blade and turn the saw on, then hold the board firmly against the miter gauge with your left hand and push the gauge forward with your right, moving the board into the blade. Caution: Keep both hands on the same side of the blade; otherwise, the board will kick back. When the board is about 2 inches beyond the blade, slide it slightly to the left and pull the miter gauge back.

To cut several pieces to the same length, clamp a wooden stop block to the table next to the rip fence at the front of the saw *(inset)*, slide the board sideways to the stop, then make the cut normally. Never use the rip fence as a stop.

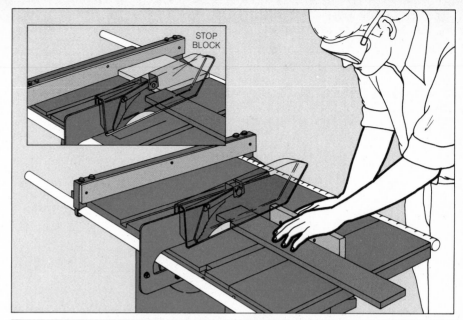

Cutting with the grain. Set the rip fence for the width of the cut. Set the board against the fence and turn the saw on, then hook two fingers of your right hand over the fence. Slowly push the board into the blade with your right hand, holding the board against the fence with your left. When your left hand is about 3 inches in front of the guard, pull it away and finish the cut with your right hand. Push the board beyond the blade and guard, then slide it to the side of the fence and pull it back.

To cut narrow pieces, 2 to 4 inches wide, finish the cut with a push stick—a notched board made from ⅜-inch plywood. For pieces less than 2 inches wide, use a notched rectangular push board made of ¾-inch plywood *(inset, left)*. To begin the cut, turn the push board upside down, hook its notched end over the rip fence and use the push board as a fence; then turn the push board over and use the notched end to complete the cut *(inset, right)*.

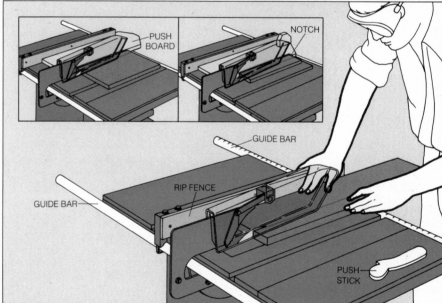

Angle cuts. Turn the head of the miter gauge to the desired angle and tighten the locking knob; the gauge ordinarily is angled toward the blade because it can cut wider boards in this position, but it also can be angled away from the blade. Align the cutting line with the blade, start the saw and push the miter gauge forward.

Hold the edge of the board tightly against the face of the gauge with both hands; otherwise the board may creep slightly and spoil the angle of the cut. If creeping persists, run wood screws partway through the miter-gauge extension; the screw points will keep the wood from sliding.

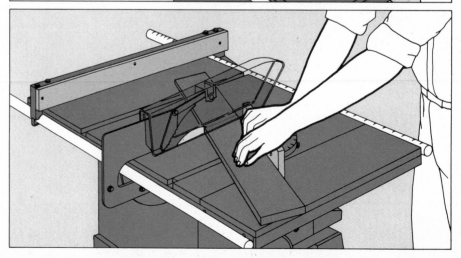

Cutting angles in wide boards. Reverse the miter gauge in its slot *(top)*, placing the head at the far side of the table. Push the board into the saw blade, holding its far edge against the gauge, until the gauge head reaches the far edge of the table. Then turn off the saw, move the gauge to the usual position, restart the saw and complete the cut *(bottom)*.

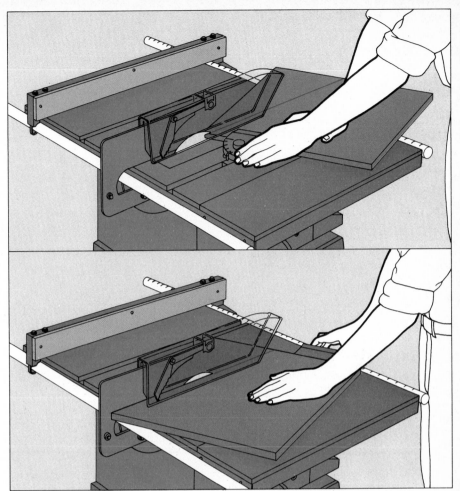

Making bevel cuts. To bevel across the grain, fit the miter gauge in the slot that the blade tilts away from, and set the gauge at 90°. Adjust the angle of the saw, using the saw's tilt scale or sighting the blade against the angle marked on the board. Hold the board against the gauge very firmly—bevel cuts tend to pull the board sideways—and make the cut the same way you would a simple crosscut.

For a compound cut *(left inset)*, set the tilt adjustment and the miter gauge to the desired angles, then cut as you would for an angle cut.

To make a bevel rip cut *(right inset)*, hold the work tightly against the rip fence and feed it as you would for a rip cut. Bevel rip cuts are best made with the rip fence on the side of the table that the blade tilts away from, if the design of your saw permits this.

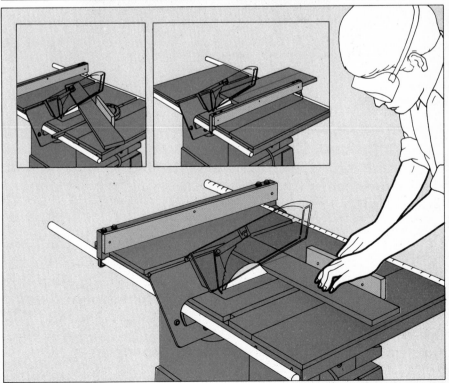

The Professional Way of Building a Cabinet

Most built-in cabinets are made in a home workshop, then fastened to the house, and for a good reason—they are better than cabinets assembled in place. In the workshop, a builder can use the strong, invisible joints that typify fine furniture and can fit the cabinets with intricate drawers and paneled doors. If you own a table saw, you naturally build in the shop, but even with portable tools, shop work is easier.

The cabinets themselves often are divided into those that hang from a wall (below) and those that are fastened to the floor (opposite), although both are made in much the same way. Each has a plywood carcass—a box consisting of top, bottom, back, sides and partitions fastened together with glue and nails (pages 26-29). To conceal the exposed plywood edges, the front of the carcass is fitted with a face frame of solid lumber 2 inches wide (pages 30-33).

The design of a cabinet is largely a matter of individual taste and needs—doors, drawers and shelves can be arranged in virtually any configuration (pages 34-37)—but a few rules of thumb do apply. The base cabinets for a kitchen are generally 36 inches high and no more than 24 inches deep; in other rooms, the depth limitation is generally 18 inches but the height depends on function and is restricted only by the height of the room ceiling. Drawers are generally no more than 24 inches wide, doors no more than 20 inches. Wall-mounted cabinets generally are about 13 inches deep, to allow easy access to the back of the cabinet; most bookcases are 10 to 12 inches deep. To prevent sagging, the length of shelves should not exceed 32 inch-

Two Basic Cabinets

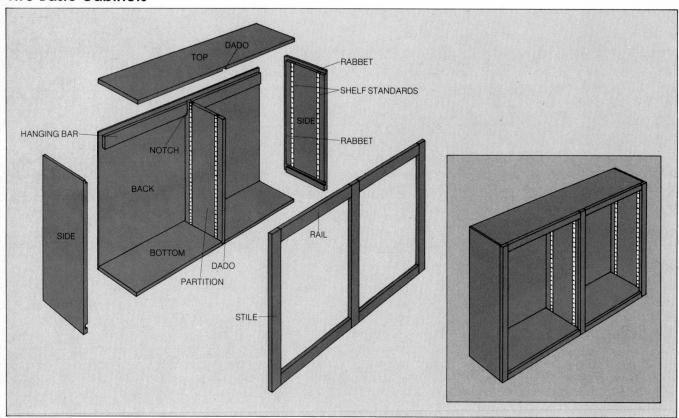

A wall-mounted cabinet. The sides, top, bottom and partition of this typical cabinet are made of ¾-inch plywood. Each side has a rabbet, or step cut, ¾ inch wide and ⅜ inch deep along its back edge; another rabbet along its top, and a dado, or groove, of the same dimensions, cut 2 inches above its bottom. The cabinet top, ¾ inch shorter than the overall length of the cabinet and ¾ inch narrower than the sides, fits into the rabbets at the tops of the sides; the bottom, cut to the same dimensions, fits into the dadoes near the bottoms of the sides. The back,

made of ¼-inch plywood, fits into the rabbets along the back edges of the sides and extends over the edges of the top and bottom; on each sidepiece, the ½ inch of rabbet protruding beyond the back is a scribing strip (page 48), used to fit the cabinet to the wall when the unit is installed. A hanging bar—a strip of ¾-inch plywood, 3 inches wide—runs across the top of the back; it ties the back of the top and sides and serves as a firm brace when the cabinet is fastened to the wall (page 27, Step 4). A center partition, ¾ inch narrower and 2 inches shorter

than the sidepieces, is notched around the bar and fits into dadoes in the top and bottom. Standards for shelves fit into dadoes in the partition and sides; the partition dadoes are offset, as in a bookcase (page 10, Step 5).

The exposed plywood edges at the front of the cabinet are covered by a face frame of solid boards ¾ inch thick and 2 inches wide (pages 30-33), with vertical stiles as long as the sides and horizontal rails fastened between the stiles with splines (pages 30-33) or dowels (page 33).

es; the width depends on their contents.

A cabinet made in a workshop and carried to its final location must be small enough to fit through the doorways, turn the corners and negotiate the stairways of the house. If the cabinet is too big to be maneuvered in one piece, or if it is longer than 8 feet—the length of a sheet of plywood—build it in sections *(page 18, top)* and fit the sections together as you install the unit. It must be possible to tilt a floor-to-ceiling cabinet upright without scraping the ceiling; the length of a diagonal measured between opposite corners on one side should be at least 1 inch less than the ceiling height.

After deciding the overall dimensions of a cabinet, sketch each piece to scale, preferably on graph paper, using 1 square of the grid per inch. On your sketch, mark the width and length of the pieces and the size and location of cuts such as dadoes, rabbets and notches *(pages 22-25)* made within a piece.

Group the pieces that use the same type of lumber—for example, sides and shelves, which require plywood with two unblemished faces of plywood; or tops and bottoms, which need only one good face. Then make a cutting sketch for each sheet of plywood. On this sketch, set pieces of the same width in a row, to be sawed with a single rip cut—allow at least ⅛ inch between pieces for the saw

kerf—and plan the use of leftover scraps for narrow, hidden parts such as the base, hanging bars and drawer supports.

Make the long rip cuts first, measuring each time from a perfectly straight edge and marking the ends of the cut with a sharp pencil; you do not have to draw a cutting line, because a table-saw fence or circular-saw guide will keep the blade straight. If you use a table saw, cut the pieces of the same width one after another, without moving the fence. For crosscuts, mark and cut the first piece of each length, then set the cut piece on each of the matching pieces and trace around it, to eliminate the errors that creep in with repeated measurements.

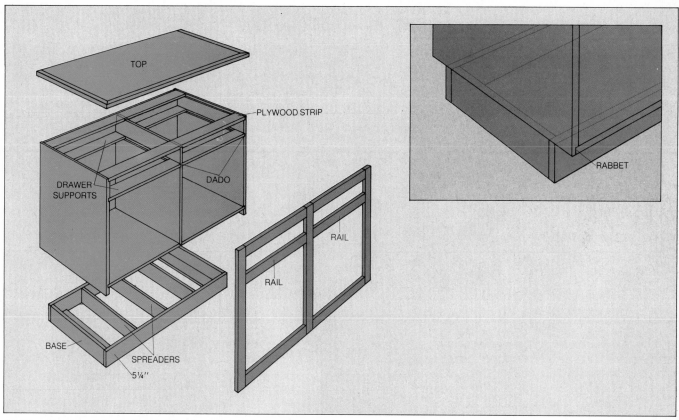

A base cabinet. A unit fastened to the floor fits together in much the same way as a wall-mounted cabinet *(opposite)*, but has several additional components. It rests on a base of ¾-inch plywood, fastened together with butt joints and reinforced with crosspieces called spreaders. The base is 5¼ inches high and is set back 3 inches from the front frame and from each exposed side of the cabinet, but the frame and side overlap the base by 1¼ inches, leaving a protective kick space 4 inches high and 3 inches deep. Exposed sides, shown here, are dadoed like

those of a wall-mounted cabinet; a side that fits against a wall or another cabinet is rabbeted, and ends flush with the bottom *(inset)*.

The back of a base cabinet is fastened directly to the wall, without a hanging bar. At the top, two horizontal strips of ¾-inch plywood, each 4 inches wide, run across the front and back, and are dadoed for a center partition. The top overhangs the cabinet by 1 inch on each side and it is fastened by short screws driven up through the plywood strips.

In a cabinet with drawers, like this one, the partition is offset slightly, so that one of its sides is flush with an edge of the center stile; when a drawer is installed, spacers are fastened to the other side of the partition and to the sides of the cabinet *(page 36, Step 1)*. At the bottom of each drawer opening, drawer supports—strips of ¾-inch plywood, 4 inches wide—are set in ⅜-inch dadoes in the sides and in ¼-inch dadoes in the partition at the front and back of the cabinet; additional rails in the face frame conceal the exposed edges of the supports.

Variations of the Basic Cabinets

A floor-to-ceiling bookcase. Elements of wall-mounted and base cabinets—a hanging bar and a plywood base—are combined in this unit, designed to be fastened to both the floor and the top of a wall. A bookcase higher than 6 feet, like this one, is reinforced with fixed shelves that fit into dadoes ¼ inch deep at or near the middle of each side and partition. The top rail of the face frame is 3 inches wide—an inch wider than the other parts of the frame; when the cabinet is installed (*page 51*), cornice molding covers 1 inch of this rail, and its exposed width matches that of the other pieces.

A floor-to-ceiling bookcase more than 6 feet wide, like this wall-to-wall unit, cannot fit through a doorway in one piece; it is actually composed of several sections, each an independent cabinet. The sections rest on a continuous base, with joints in the frontpieces and backpieces made between spreaders and reinforced by concealed cleats. The cabinet sections are screwed together when the bookcase is installed (*page 49, Step 1*).

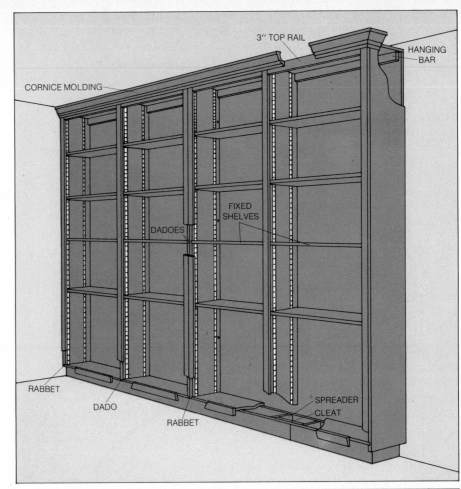

A room divider. Open on both sides, a see-through base cabinet can be built with a countertop that juts out from a wall, as in this example, or as a ceiling-high partition between two areas. The countertop of a 36-inch cabinet overhangs each side by 1 inch; the top of a floor-to-ceiling cabinet is finished like that of a wall-mounted cabinet (*page 16*), and a fixed shelf (*above*) is added near the middle of the unit.

A room divider is generally about 24 inches deep, permitting easy access to the shelves from either face of the unit. Structural rigidity is provided by frames fastened to both faces of the unit, rather than by a single face frame and a conventional plywood back.

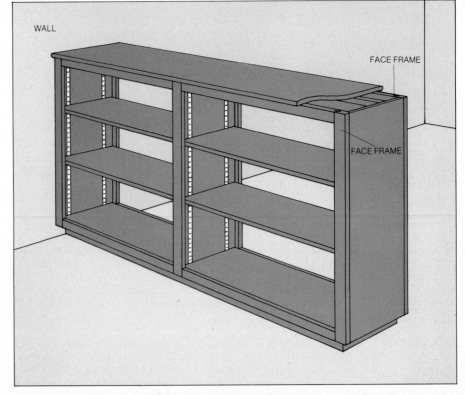

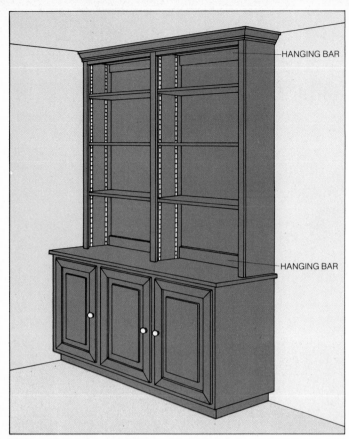

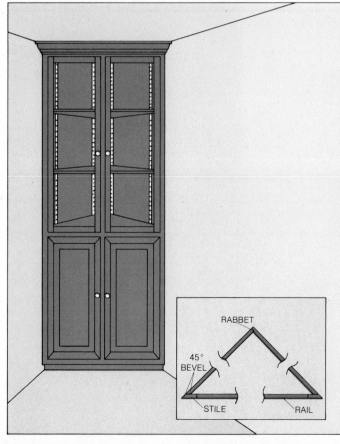

A cabinet and bookcase combined. The cabinet of this unit, generally about 32 inches high and 18 inches deep, is built in the usual way *(page 17)*; the bookcase, generally as wide as the base and about 12 inches deep, resembles a wall-mounted cabinet, but has a second hanging bar rather than a plywood sheet at the bottom. The sides of the bookcase bear on those of the cabinet, 1 inch inside the edges of the cabinet top, and the sections are fastened together in the course of installation *(page 49, Step 1)*.

An island cabinet. This kitchen cabinet, commonly set beneath an overhead island unit, is generally 36 inches high and 3 to 4 feet deep. A partition runs from front to back, and a ¾-inch false back fits into dadoes at the middle of the partition, sides and bottom. As in a room divider, face frames are installed on both front and back.

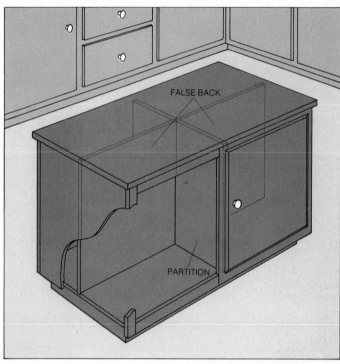

A triangular corner cabinet. The parts of this unit, traditionally used as a china hutch or display cabinet, are laid out like those of the corner cabinet on pages 10-12, but fit together differently. The sides meet in a rabbet joint at the rear *(inset)* and are dadoed for a fixed shelf. At the front, the edges of the sides have 45° bevels that fit flush with the top and bottom, and the edges of the face frame are beveled to fit flush against the walls. In the popular design shown here, two types of doors *(page 37)* are used: paneled doors, which provide access to storage space at the bottom, and glass doors, which protect the display shelves at the top.

19

Cutting the Parts with a Portable Saw

Two self-aligning jigs. To cut sheets of plywood with the grain, make a jig from two 8-foot strips of ¾-inch plywood. Cut one 4 inches wide so that you retain a factory-cut edge, and screw it to the second strip, 12 inches wide, with the factory-cut edge inside and the other along one edge of the wide strip. Clamp the pieces to a workbench with the wide piece on the bottom and overhanging the edge of the bench, set the saw on the wide piece, and use the factory-cut edge of the narrow piece as a guide to cut a strip from the wide one.

Make a jig for crosscutting in the same way, but use strips of plywood 30 inches long.

Making the cuts. Set two 2-by-4s about 3 feet apart on a pair of sawhorses and place the cabinet plywood, good face down, on the 2-by-4s. Align the cut edge of the jig with the cutting marks at each end of the plywood, clamp the jig to the panel, and set the toe of the saw against the guide with the blade ⅛ inch deeper than the bottom of the panel. Start the saw and push the blade slowly through the board, holding the base plate tight against the guide. Be sure that both pieces are well supported at the end of the cut, otherwise they will bind on the blade.

FACTORY-CUT EDGE

Working with Panels on a Table Saw

Ripping long pieces. Adjust the rip fence in the correct position for the cut and set the blade ⅛ inch higher than the thickness of the panel, then rest the end of the sheet on the edge of the table and have a helper turn the saw on. While you hold the sheet perfectly level, have your helper push it tight against the rip fence; now slowly feed it through the blade. At the middle of the cut have your helper move to the far side of the table to support the cut pieces as they slide off the table; the helper should not try to lift them up or pull them through the saw. Finish the cut as you would an ordinary rip cut (*page 14, middle*), and when both pieces are beyond the blade, have the helper pull them off the table.

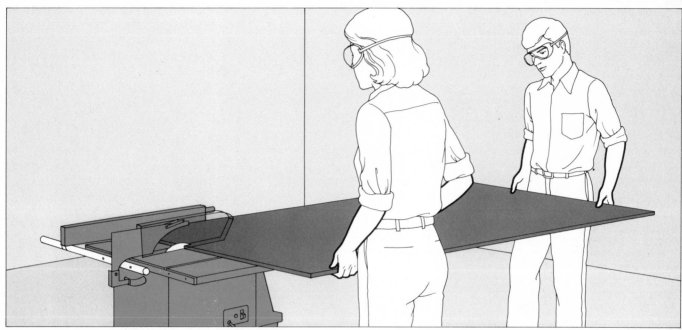

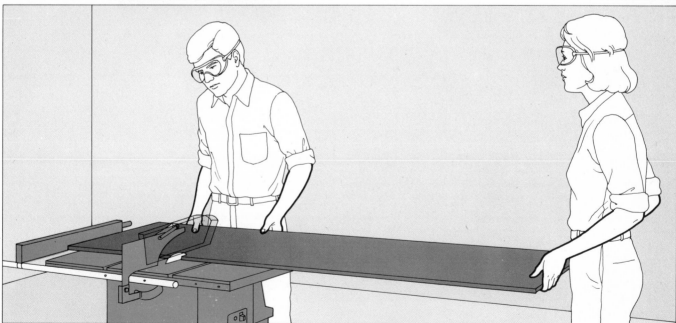

Crosscutting plywood sheets. To cut a piece more than 18 inches wide, treat the cut as a rip cut: adjust the rip fence for the length of the cut, set the edge of the board on the table in front of the blade and, if the board is more than 4 feet long, have a helper support the end of the board. Slowly feed the board through the blade, holding it tight against the rip fence. Caution: Because this technique is an exception to the basic safety rules for a table saw—it uses the rip fence for a crosscut—it increases the danger of a kickback. Keep the board perfectly square and make sure your helper supports its weight without moving it sideways. To cut pieces less than 18 inches wide, fit the miter gauge with a long extension and reverse it in its slot (*page 15, top*); make the first part of the cut with the miter gauge located on the far side of the board; then, halfway through the board, turn the saw off and return the gauge to the normal position to complete the cut.

The Craft of Cutting Joints

The pieces of the cabinets shown on pages 16-19 fit together in tight interlocking joints. Some of the joints are made at grooves called dadoes, others at stepped edges called rabbets; both kinds are generally ¾ inch wide and ⅜ inch deep. These classic woodworking joints strengthen a cabinet by increasing the gluing area, and they make the pieces easy to assemble and align. The strength of the joints themselves depends on the precision of the tool that makes the cuts.

A router fitted with a ¾-inch straight bit makes both dado and rabbet cuts with razor-sharp precision. To run the cuts in a perfectly straight line, you will need a straightedge guide *(right)*. Hold the router firmly—it tends to twist away from you—start every cut with the bit clear of the wood and move the router at a moderate speed from left to right.

Because a router is portable and can be set anywhere on the work, it is especially suited for cutting hard-to-reach dadoes, such as those in a fixed shelf in the middle of a tall cabinet or bookcase. At other locations a table saw does the job in less time with about the same degree of precision. General techniques for the table saw are described on pages 13-15.

To make dado and rabbet cuts with a table saw, you can fit it with a one-blade assembly called a wobbler, or with a more precise accessory called a dado head, consisting of a set of blades of different thicknesses. The width of a dado-head cut is determined by the number of inner blades, or "chippers"; on most models, fine adjustments of the width are made with paper washers inserted between the chippers. A homemade attachment called a featherboard, fitted to the rip fence of the saw, holds the stock down and against the blade. When the saw is used to cut rabbets, an additional jig—a wooden fence with a rounded notch *(page 24, Step 4)*—prevents the blade from touching the metal fence.

Whichever tool you use, begin by grouping the cabinet pieces that need matching joints, using your working drawings to determine the cuts for each piece. Mark the position and width of each cut, using one piece as a template to mark those with duplicate joints. If you are using a router, mark guidelines *(right)* the same way. Use your template as a sample: Make the cuts it requires, then recheck the position of the marked cuts on other pieces in the same group.

If you use a table saw, set the blade and rip fence for one cut and cut all pieces with the same joint before resetting the blade and fence. On each piece, cut the rabbet joints first. Double-check the positions of the dadoes, using the inside edges of the rabbets as reference points, then cut the dadoes that run across the wood grain. Finish by cutting the dadoes that run with the grain.

Making Dadoes and Rabbets with a Router

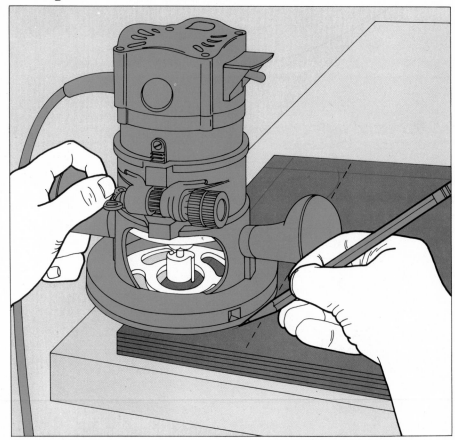

Positioning a guide. Mark the positions and widths of the dadoes and rabbets on the board, using two lines for a dado, one for a rabbet. Set the router bit flush with the base, and place the router near the board edge that is to be cut, with the bit centered in the marked dado or rabbet. Trace the outline of the router base, trace a second outline near the opposite edge of the board and, using a straightedge, draw a guideline between the router-base outlines at the points farthest from the cutting lines for the dado or rabbet.

Sand and wax the edge of a straight piece of plywood that is 6 inches wide and is cut to the length of the joint. Fasten the marked board to a workbench, using a C clamp and, if necessary, a sixpenny nail driven partway. Set the waxed edge of the guide along the guideline and clamp or nail the guide to the board.

Cutting a rabbet. After fastening the board and guide in place, set the base of the router on the board, with the bit clear of the wood and 2 inches in from the left end. Turn the power on and push the bit into the wood, toward the rabbet line, until the base of the router meets the edge of the guide; then move the router from left to right, pressing it firmly against the guide. Complete the cut by moving the router from right to left through the uncut 2 inches of the rabbet.

Cutting a dado. Place the router with its base against the guide and its bit clear of the left edge of the wood. Turn the power on, push the bit into the wood and move the router along the guide until the bit clears the right edge of the board.

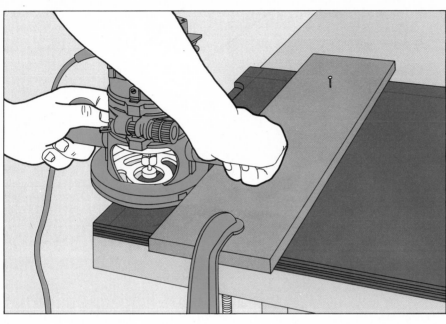
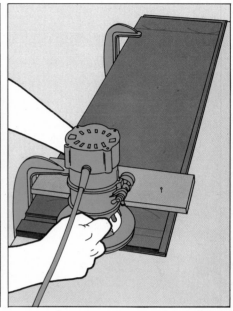

A Dado Head on a Table Saw

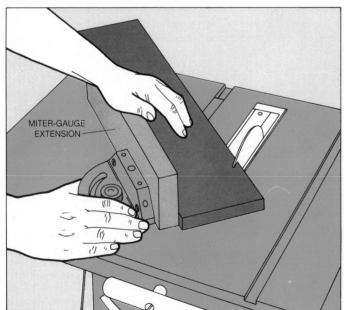

MITER-GAUGE EXTENSION

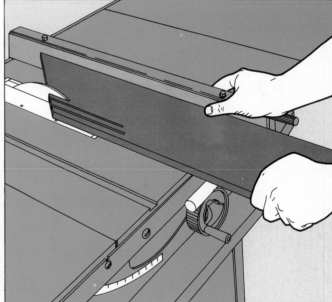

1 Mitering the featherboard. Use the table saw as shown on pages 13-15 to cut a piece of solid wood ¾ inch thick, 2 feet long and 5 inches wide for the featherboard; then fit the miter gauge with a smooth wood extension, set the gauge at a 45° angle and hold the cut board against the extension with your left hand. Start the saw; push the gauge forward with your right hand to cut the wood about 5 inches in from the end.

2 Slotting the featherboard. Remove the miter gauge, fasten the rip fence 4¾ inches from the blade and cut a slot 5 inches deep in the mitered end of the featherboard. Cut identical slots at ¼-inch intervals, moving the fence ¼ inch closer to the blade before each cut.

3 **Attaching the dado head.** With the table saw unplugged, remove the standard blade and table insert, install an outside blade of the dado head on the arbor and add chippers and, if necessary, paper washers to bring the interior of the head to the correct width. Set the other outside blade on the arbor, replace the arbor washer and screw the arbor nut loosely in place.

Adjust the blades so that the larger teeth of one outside blade are opposite the smaller teeth of the other, and the chippers line up with gullets of both blades *(inset)*, then tighten the arbor nut. Install a wide-slotted dado insert in the saw table.

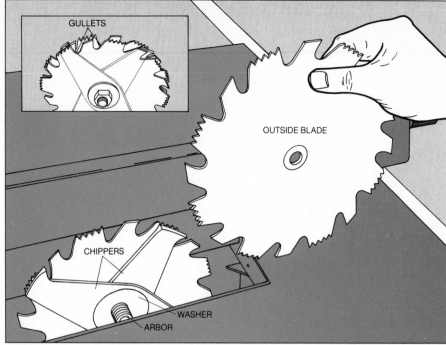

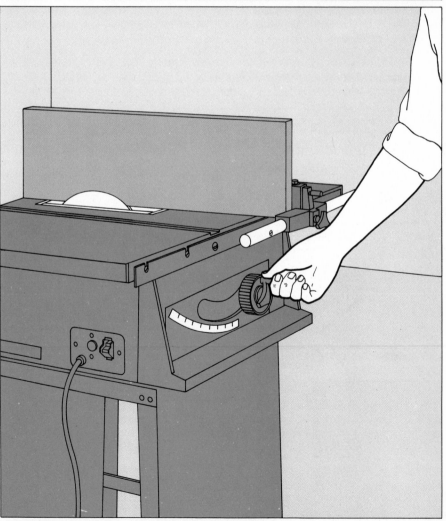

4 **Notching a fence for the rabbet cuts.** Lower the dado head to the level of the table. Fit the metal rip fence with a wooden auxiliary fence 6 inches high and ¾ inch thick, and position the wooden fence so that ¼ inch of its thickness overlaps the dado head; then turn the power on and slowly raise the dado head about ½ inch to cut a rounded notch in the wooden fence. Turn off the power and retract the blade.

5 **Setting up the featherboard.** Place a piece of scrap lumber as thick as the cabinet pieces on the table against the fence. Clamp the featherboard to the fence with its slotted edge resting on the scrap board and its tip 2 inches from the edge of the rounded notch in the fence. Check the setting of the featherboard by moving the scrap forward along the fence; the ''feathers'' should snap back and forth. Raise the dado head and test-cut a rabbet ⅜ inch deep.

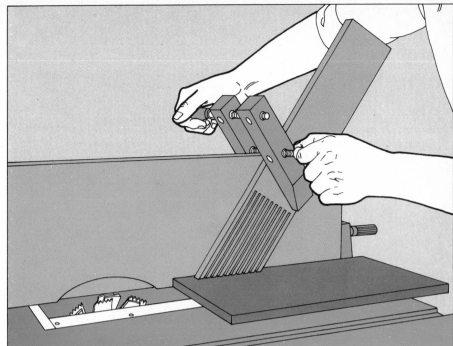

6 **Making the cuts.** To cut a rabbet *(right)*, turn the power on, set the cabinet piece on the infeed side of the table, with its edge against the fence and beneath the featherboard, and slowly push the board forward over the dado head. Cut a dado near the edge of a board in the same way, but position the fence as for a rip cut.

To cut a dado in the middle of a board *(below, right)*, clamp a wooden stop block to the table or to the rip fence near the front of the saw to set the location of the dado; then fit the miter gauge with an auxiliary fence. Turn the power on, place the board on the infeed side of the table and with its edge against the stop block; push the gauge forward slowly toward the dado head with your right hand, holding the board firmly down and against the gauge with your left.

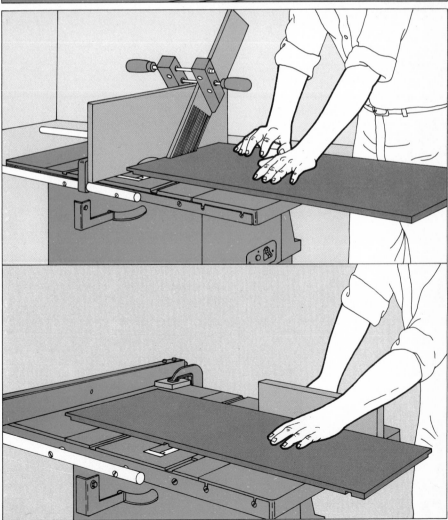

Putting the Pieces Together

Wall-mounted and base cabinets are assembled in much the same way, though a base cabinet requires a few additional steps *(pages 28-29)*. After the parts have been dadoed and rabbeted *(pages 22-25)*, they are assembled face down on the workshop floor over protective sheets of cardboard or scrap plywood, and fastened together with white carpenter's glue and finishing nails. The entire job must be done within two or three hours, so that the pieces are aligned and the back installed before the glue sets.

A twist in a piece may keep it from fitting neatly into a dado; if necessary, enlist a helper to pop the joint together, or make braces to force the bowed piece straight *(page 29, top)*. If the joints are somewhat loose—nominal ¾-inch plywood may actually be only ¹¹/₁₆ inch thick—you can wedge them tight with thin wooden shims tapped into the hidden side of the joints; for more precise joints, measure the thickness of the plywood before you cut the joint so that you can adjust the width of the dadoes and rabbets accordingly.

The vagaries of plywood can cause a third problem: Nails driven into plywood edges occasionally hit knots—which can deflect a nail through the finished face of the cabinet—or a hollow spot. Do not attempt to drive the nail or correct its course: Pull it out and use another one about an inch away.

Assembling a Wall-mounted Cabinet

1 Test-fitting the pieces. Have a helper hold a cabinet side on edge on the floor, front down, while you slide the bottom into its dado; if necessary, hold a block of lumber against the plywood over the dado and tap the block with a hammer to slide the dado home. Set the bottom into its dado in the other side, slide the top into the rabbets in the sides, then slide the partition into its dadoes in the top and bottom. Measure the actual dimensions of the cabinet and inspect the joints; if the dimensions are wrong, recut the parts.

Take the cabinet apart and mark lines across the top, bottom and sides, opposite the middle of each dado. Starting 1 inch from the end of each dado, start sixpenny finishing nails along the lines every 4 inches.

2 Fastening the carcass. Squeeze ⅛-inch beads of glue in the dado in one side and onto the end of the cabinet bottom and slide the two pieces together, front edges on the floor. Drive the nails started in Step 1 into the bottom, then glue and nail the other side to the bottom. If the cabinet will be painted, wipe off any excess glue immediately with a wet rag; if it will be stained, let the glue dry for 15 minutes and pare it off with a sharp chisel.

Apply glue beads to the rabbet at the top of each side and to the ends of the top, slide these pieces tightly together and drive nails through the top into the sides *(inset)*; if the top of the cabinet will be covered by molding or a soffit *(pages 50-51)*, also nail through the side into the end of the top. Finally, apply glue to the ends of the partition and to its dadoes in the top and bottom, slide it down into the dadoes and drive nails (started in Step 1) into its ends.

3 Squaring the cabinet. Working with a helper, hook the end of a steel tape ruler on one corner of the cabinet and measure diagonally to the opposite corner; measure the other diagonal in the same way. If the measurements differ, push the corners used for the longer measurement toward each other and let them spring back, then remeasure both diagonals. Repeat the adjustment until the measurements are equal, then set all the nails.

Cut a hanging bar—a piece of ¾-inch plywood, 4 inches wide—to fit snugly between the sidepieces and start two sixpenny nails in each sidepiece opposite the ends of the hanging bar.

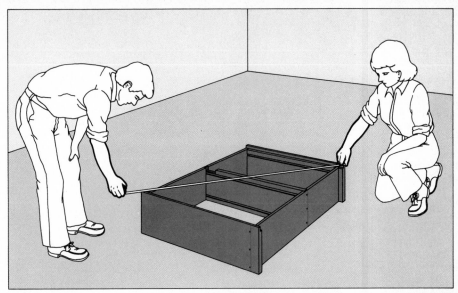

4 Installing the hanging bar. Apply glue beads to the top and ends of the hanging bar and to the areas it will meet at the top of the cabinet and the partition, slide the bar into place and drive the nails started in Step 3. Drive two nails through the bar into the partition, and nail through the cabinet top into the bar every 6 inches.

HANGING BAR

5 Aligning the cabinet. Make sure the cabinet is square (*Step 3*)—adjust it if necessary; then sight from the top edge of one sidepiece to the edge of the other near each corner. If one corner is higher than the others (*inset*), because of a twist in the cabinet or an irregularity in the floor, raise the low corners on shingle shims.

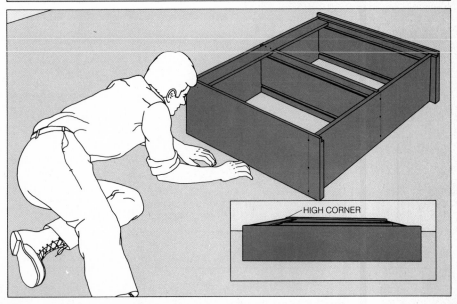

HIGH CORNER

6 **Attaching the back.** Glue and nail a ¼-inch plywood back cut to fit between the outer edges of the top and bottom and between the rabbets in the sides. Apply the glue to the sides, top, bottom, partition and hanging bar, but not to the back itself; use 1⅛-inch flathead nails, driven through the back at 3-inch intervals into the sides, top, bottom and partition, with the side nails angled slightly outward. Drive two rows of nails through the back into the hanging bar.

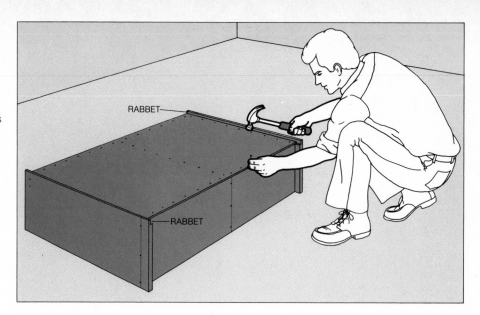

The Specialized Parts of a Base Cabinet

Making the base. Nail together a base of front and back pieces, end pieces, and interior braces called spreaders. For the front and back, use 5¼-inch strips of ¾-inch plywood cut to the length of the cabinet if both ends will be concealed by walls, cut 3 inches shorter if one end is exposed, and cut 6 inches shorter if both are exposed. For the ends and spreaders, use strips 4½ inches less than the cabinet width for a standard cabinet, 7½ inches less for an island cabinet or room divider. Nail the ends, front and back together, then nail a spreader beneath each partition and a spreader between partitions. At each end set a 4-inch horizontal screwing strip of ¾-inch plywood flush with the top and nail it to the front, back and sidepieces.

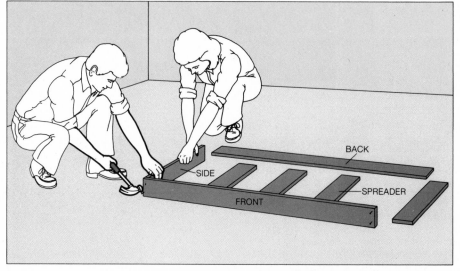

Installing drawer supports. Before installing the cabinet back (*page 28, Step 6*), nail drawer-support strips of ¾-inch plywood, 4 inches wide, between the dadoes in the sides and partition. Working down from the top of the cabinet, fasten a strip below each drawer opening, flush with the cabinet front, using glue and two sixpenny nails at each end; then fasten another strip flush with the back edge.

If the drawer supports fit into matching dadoes on both sides of a partition (*inset*), fasten the strips on one side with fourpenny nails driven straight into their ends, then fasten the strips on the other side with fourpenny nails toenailed through the support strip, into the partition.

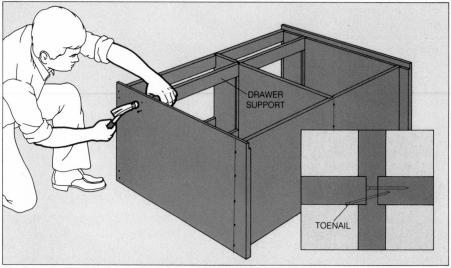

Temporary braces for fixed shelves. After installing the fixed shelves for a floor-to-ceiling cabinet by the method described (*opposite, bottom*), tap a brace of lumber—a scrap of 1-by-2 will do—between the cabinet bottom and the middle of the shelf; to determine the length of the brace, measure the distance between the bottom and an end of the shelf. Measure between the cabinet top and the ends of the shelves, cut braces to these lengths and fit them between the top and the middle of each shelf. Install the cabinet back (*page 28, Step 6*), fastening it to the shelves with glue and with sixpenny nails every 6 inches, then remove the braces.

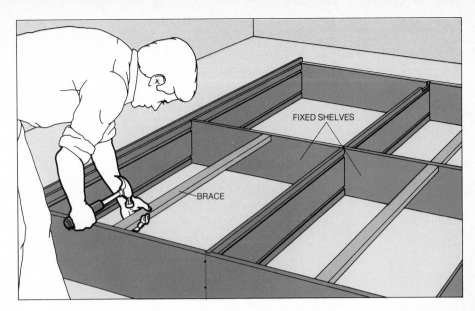

Making a Countertop

1 Installing the supports. After fastening the bottom to the sides (*page 26, Step 2*), glue and nail two 4-inch strips of ¾-inch plywood between the rabbets at the tops of the sides. Prepare these strips by cutting matching dadoes for the partition across the middle of each strip; set a strip flush with the front edge, and glue and nail it to the sides (*page 26, Step 2, inset*). Install the other strip flush with the back of the cabinet, then install the partition.

For a wooden countertop, cut a piece of plywood ¼ inch longer and wider than the finished cabinet and face frame. For a countertop that will be covered with plastic laminate, cut a piece of plywood 1 inch wider than the cabinet and 1 inch longer at each exposed side, and glue and nail ¾-inch butt-jointed battens (made of plywood or 1-inch dimension lumber) to the bottom of the plywood, flush with each edge (*inset*); nail the battens in a zigzag pattern.

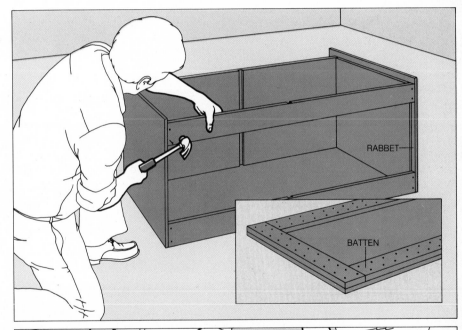

2 Completing a wooden countertop. Set a length of wooden nosing, ¾ inch thick, 1 inch wide and miter cut at one end, against the longest exposed edge of the top, with the miter at an exposed corner, and mark the location of the other corner on the nosing. Make a miter cut at the mark if the side is exposed, a square cut if it adjoins a wall. Fasten the nosing to the edge with glue and fourpenny finishing nails driven through pilot holes every 6 inches. Mark, cut and fasten nosings to the other exposed sides; the back edge and any side edge that adjoins a wall do not need nosing because the plywood will be scribed to fit the wall (*page 48, bottom*).

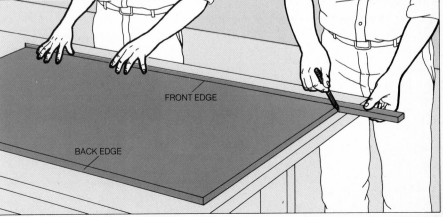

The Final Step: A Face Frame

Two Ways to Build a Frame

Covering the unfinished plywood edges at the front of a well-built cabinet is a face frame of solid lumber, ¾ inch thick and 2 inches wide—pine or poplar for cabinets that will be painted, birch for stained cabinets, and occasionally fine hardwoods such as cherry and oak. A lumberyard or mill will plane the boards to a uniform width and thickness; you must cut the pieces to length, fasten them with glue and wooden splines or dowels, and nail them on.

Cut with special precision, for tiny errors multiply as successive cuts are made. Follow a pencil sketch based on the measurements of each piece of the cabinet carcass—the plywood top and sides of the cabinet without its face frame. To saw the pieces, use a stop *(page 14, top, inset)* rather than a guideline. To calculate the lengths of the frame pieces, follow these rules:

☐ The top of the top rail should be flush with the carcass top.

☐ The top of the bottom rail should be flush with the carcass floor.

☐ Side stiles generally are 1¼ inches longer than the height of the carcass.

☐ The outside of an exposed stile should be flush with the carcass side.

☐ A stile that meets a wall should overhang the carcass side at least ½ inch to provide a scribing strip *(page 48)*; if a bank of drawers will be installed next to this stile, align the inside edge of the stile flush with the inside edge of the carcass.

☐ In a cabinet with drawers, the center partition is generally offset ⅝ inch and the center stile is set flush with one side of the partition.

☐ Intermediate rails are set flush with the top of the drawer supports.

The simplest way to fasten the face frame together is with splines—thin pieces of wood that fit into hidden slots in the ends and edges of the boards. This method leaves a slight margin for error and permits some adjustments after the joints are cut. The slots are made with a router and a special slotting bit, which cuts a groove ¾ or ½ inch deep and ⅛ inch wide. Splines can be ordered from a mill or cut with a table saw. If you use the saw, rip ¾-inch boards into strips that fit snugly when gently tapped into the

slots with a hammer; hold several strips together and crosscut them into pieces twice the depth of the slots, less 1/16 inch.

Stronger than splines are dowels—birch pegs glued into holes in the joining pieces. Dowels pregrooved with spiral glue channels are available from lumberyards. Dowel construction does not permit adjustments after the frame is assembled. The holes for the dowels must be marked perfectly and drilled squarely, with the help of an accurate doweling jig.

A frame easy to cut. In this frame only two lengths of wood are used; all stiles are one length, all rails another. The pieces are joined by thin wooden strips called splines that are glued into slots in the mating pieces. Where one side of a joint will be hidden from view—as by a countertop—the mating slots run out the end of the stile and out the hidden side of the rail and are connected by two splines *(top inset)*. If both sides of a joint are visible—as at the end of an intermediate rail—a "blind" joint is made with slots shorter than the rail width, connected by a single spline *(bottom inset)*. Dowels *(bottom of page)* can also be used to join this frame.

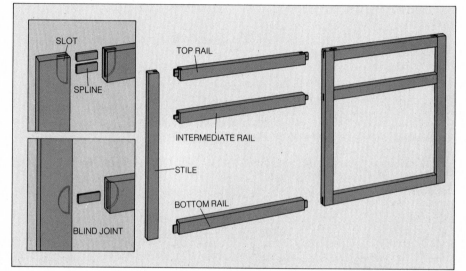

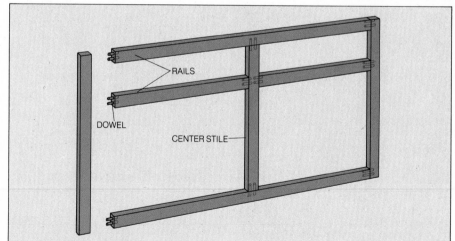

A frame with minimum joints. This design, which requires two fewer joints than the frame at the top of this page, is generally preferred for a cabinet that will be stained—staining leaves the joints visible, and the fewer the joints, the easier it is to achieve an attractive finish. The top and bottom rails run between the side stiles and a short center stile fits between the rails. At each

joint of this frame, two 5/16-inch dowels, 2 inches long, are glued into precisely aligned holes in the end of one piece and the edge of the other, fastening the two pieces together.

Splined joints should not be used with this design because blind joints would have to be made for the center stile, weakening the frame.

Making a Frame with Spline Joints

1 Marking two pieces. After cutting the stiles and the top and bottom rails, assemble them face up on the workbench; mark an X on the face of each board and matching letters on the sides of each joint. Draw lines on the edge of each stile to mark the inside corners made by stile and rails.

If your cabinet will have intermediate rails to conceal drawer supports or fixed shelves, measure from the top of the carcass to the top of each support, mark the measured distance down from the top of a stile and mark the stile for the top and bottom of each intermediate rail. Set the other stiles beside the marked one and transfer the marks to them with a combination square (*inset*), then reassemble the frame with the intermediate rails and mark the stile edges at the corners made by these rails.

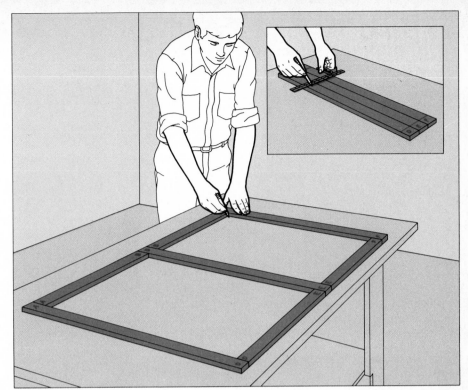

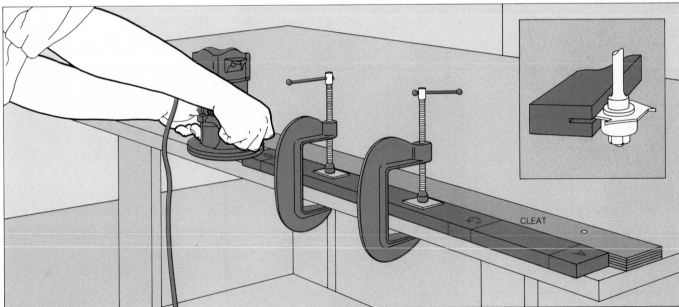

2 Slotting the stiles. Cut a slot in the stiles for each rail-to-stile joint, using a router fitted with a three-cutter spline bit that makes a groove ⅛ inch wide and ¾ or ½ inch deep.

To hold the stiles down, nail a scrap of lumber 1¾ inches from the edge of a workbench; clamp a stile face up beside this cleat; the stile will overhang the workbench edge. Adjust the router depth to cut the slot in the middle of the stile thickness, then turn the router on and, beginning at the left end of the stile, move the router slowly from left to right to make a shallow cut;

stop the cut about ⅛ inch short of the mark for the edge of the rail. Make two or three more passes until the guide of the bit rolls on the edge of the stile (*inset*).

At the right end of the board, start the slot by easing the bit into the middle of the stile thickness just within the line you have marked for the edge of the rail, then make several shallow passes with the router as you did at the other end of the board. Slot the other stiles in the same way, always moving the router from left to right. To make a blind slot for a spline joint in an intermedi-

ate rail, cut a slot that does not extend beyond the marks that indicate the edges of the rail.

To slot the rails, clamp each rail, face up, against the cleat with the end to be cut overhanging the table. Move the router very slowly from left to right, in several shallow passes—the end grain of rails is difficult to cut and can overheat the bit. If the left edge of the rail will be exposed, ease the bit into the end of the board about ⅛ inch from the edge and cut to the right corner; if the right edge will be exposed, start at the left corner and stop the cut just short of the edge.

3 **Inserting splines into rails.** Squeeze a glue bead into the slots of each rail, then cover the splines with a thin coat of glue and tap them into the rail with a hammer. If the slot runs through one edge of the rail, as it does at a corner, set one spline flush with the edge and another inside it; for a blind slot, set one spline in the slot. Let the glue set for about 15 minutes.

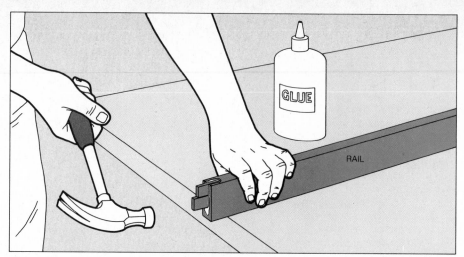

4 **Splining rails to stiles.** Fasten each rail to one of the side stiles by first applying glue to one of the end slots of the stile and additional glue to the splines at the end of the matching rail. Then set the stile on edge and work the splines partway into the stile by rocking the rail from side to side. Set a block of wood on the other end of the rail and tap the rail home with a hammer.

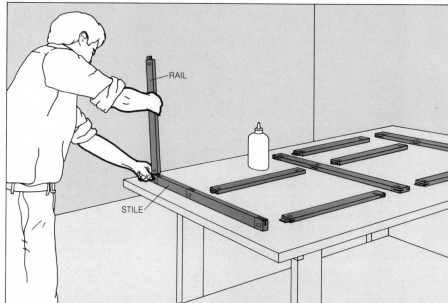

5 **Completing the joints.** After applying a coat of glue to the splines at the free ends of the rails and a bead to the slots in the center stile, fit the stile onto the splines. Have a helper hold the rails steady while you rock the stile partway onto the splines; then, working from one end, tap the stile onto the rails with a hammer and a block of wood. Set the completed section of the face frame on the floor, install the remaining rails in the center stile, then install the remaining side stile as you did the center one (above).

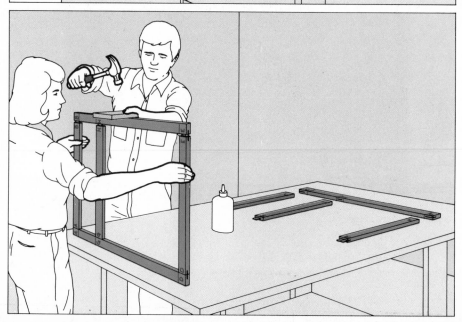

6 **Clamping the frame.** Set the frame across a workbench, overhanging each side, and fasten bar clamps around the outer stiles, directly over the top and bottom rails; protect the stiles with scraps of wood. Tighten the clamps until glue is forced out of the joints, then measure the diagonals of the frame (page 27, Step 3) to make sure it is square; if it is not, reset the clamps at a slight angle to the rails to pull the frame into square. When the frame is square, sight across the top for twists; if necessary, pull the low corner sharly to bring it into line. When the cabinet is square and properly aligned, back off about a quarter turn on each clamp.

If your frame has intermediate rails, turn the clamped frame over, rest the clamps on the workbench and fasten an additional clamp across each intermediate rail.

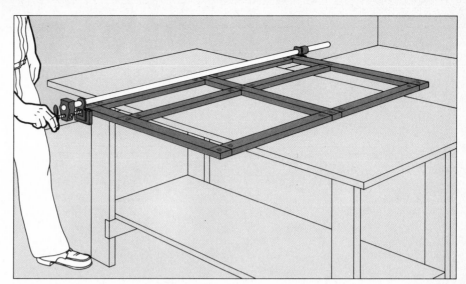

7 **Nailing the frame in place.** Set the carcass of the cabinet flat on its back, set the frame in place and check the fit, particularly at exposed edges. If the frame projects beyond edges that should be flush, plane the wood to fit after installation. If the frame is too small, either line it up at the edge that gets the most exposure, or build another frame.

Glue the frame to the plywood edges of the carcass. Drill pilot holes and fasten the frame with sixpenny finishing nails every 6 inches, starting at a corner where the frame and carcass must line up—for example, the bottom corner at an exposed end. Check the alignment of the frame and carcass before you drive each nail; if the plywood is bowed, force it straight with your hand or with bar clamps. Work along each side and do not drive nails at the far corner until the side is completed. After the outer sides, nail the center stile and the intermediate rails. Then set the nails and plane the edges if necessary.

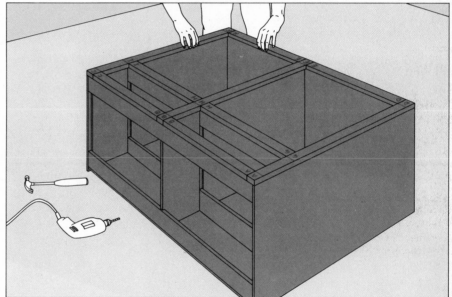

Drilling for Doweled Joints

Marking the holes. After marking the joints (page 31, Step 1), set the side stiles side by side, with the joint marks upward; clamp the stiles together and mark their edges for the hole centers. Draw lines across all of the edges simultaneously with a combination square, ½ and 1½ inches from each end; mark for intermediate rails ½ inch from each rail edge. Clamp the rails together in the same way, and mark across the ends, ½ inch from each edge; if a stile runs into the center of a rail, mark the joint as you marked the stiles with intermediate rails.

Center a doweling jig on each mark and drill a $^5/_{16}$-inch hole 1⅛ inches deep with a brad-point bit. Glue dowels into the holes and assemble rails and stiles as for splines (pages 31-33).

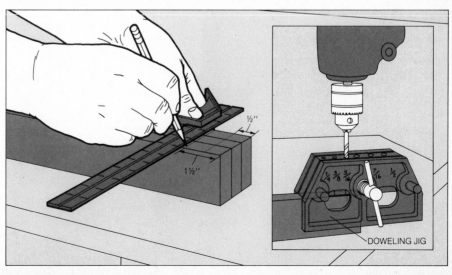

DOWELING JIG

Fitting a Cabinet with Drawers and Doors

Doors and drawers transform shelves into a finished cabinet. A door *(pages 37-41)* encloses the cabinet; a set of drawers organizes its space and makes its contents accessible. As the only moving parts of a typical cabinet, both drawers and doors are subject to unusual stresses and so must be constructed with strong joints and sturdy materials.

The materials that are generally used for making drawer backs and sides are plywood or lumber at least ½ inch thick; bottoms are plywood or hardboard at least ¼ inch thick; and fronts are plywood or lumber ¾ inch thick. These pieces can be put together in a variety of ways, using any type of connection from the simple butt joint to the sophisticated dovetail joint. The majority of built-in drawers use a compromise between these two extremes—a standardized pattern of rabbets and dadoes that can be cut with a router, a table saw *(opposite)* or even a handsaw and chisel.

The technique of drawer construction also is influenced by the style of the drawer front. The simplest to make and the most commonly employed is the lipped drawer front, which has a rabbeted edge that overlaps the cabinet frame. Because the overlap conceals any irregularities of fit between the drawer and its opening, this type of drawer requires no finicky sanding and planing.

Less common because of the difficulty of achieving the exact fit required is the flush drawer, whose front fits inside the cabinet so that the cabinet surface remains smooth, uninterrupted by projections. For this style you must cut the front precisely to the size of the drawer opening and then painstakingly trim it with a block plane and sandpaper to create equal clearances of 1/16 inch all around the drawer. If you install both doors and drawers in a single cabinet or a set of cabinets, use the same style, overlapping or flush, for both.

Drawers stronger than those ordinarily constructed can be made by altering the rabbeting. Rabbeting the sides to hold an unrabbeted front, for example, creates a stronger joint and adds rigidity, but requires that you glue and screw a false front to the drawer to cover the end grain of the sides. For an even stronger joint

between front and sides, use the so-called double dado *(right, inset)*, which also requires a false front.

The mechanism that guides a drawer's movement is critical to the overall dimensions of the drawer. Traditionally the drawers in fine furniture slide on wooden runners, but in modern built-in cabinets commercial metal glides are generally preferred for their sturdiness and ease of

installation. Glides require extra space—specified by the manufacturer but generally ½ inch—between the drawer sides and the opening edges, and the drawer front must extend beyond the sides to conceal the hardware.

In the course of construction, test-fit drawer pieces and check them for squareness before you glue, clamp and nail the joints together.

Basic Drawer Designs

The lipped drawer. Fit the bottom into side and front dadoes cut ¼ inch deep and located ½ inch above the lower edges of the frame. The back rests on the bottom and fits into vertical side dadoes ¼ inch deep, set ½ inch in from the back edges. The drawer front—cut ½ inch larger on each side than the opening—is rabbeted on all edges. Rabbets holding the drawer sides have a depth equal to two thirds the thickness of the front, and a width calculated by adding ⅜ inch (for overlap) to the thickness of a sidepiece plus the thickness of the glide hardware. Rabbets along the top and bottom of the front are the same depth as the end rabbets, but only ⅜ inch wide. The joints are held by glue and by fourpenny nails driven at an angle through the sides and back edge of the bottom.

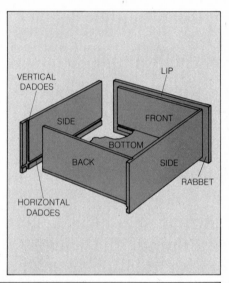

An extra-strength drawer. A two-layer front adds rigidity; a construction front fits into ¼-inch-deep rabbets cut along the front edges of the sides, and a false front is glued and screwed over the construction front. The drawer back, as

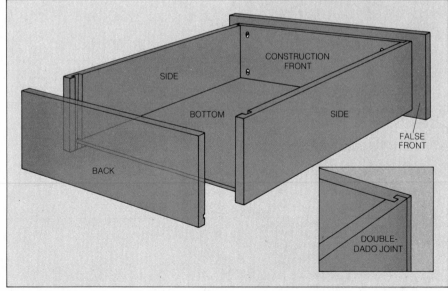

well as the front and sides, is grooved for the drawer bottom. For an especially strong joint between the construction front and the sides, you can cut a double dado *(inset and opposite)* instead of rabbeting the sides to receive the front.

A Double-Dado Joint for Extra Strength

1 Dadoing the sides. If you are using a table saw, mount a ¼-inch dado head (*page 24*) and clamp a stop block on a miter-gauge extension; when you butt a drawer side against the block, the left edge of the dado head should be ½ inch from the end of the drawer side. Set the dado-head height at 5/16 inch, hold the drawer side with its inside face down, and cut the dado. Similarly cut the opposite drawer side.

If you use a router (*pages 22-23*) to cut the dadoes, fit it with a ¼-inch bit, set the bit 5/16 inch deep and use a jig to guide the bit ½ inch from the front end of the side.

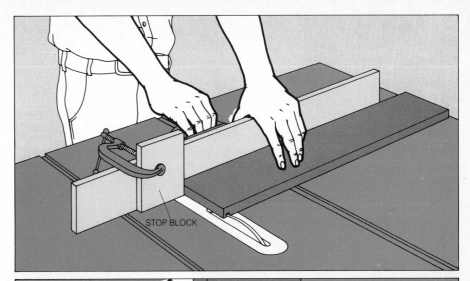

STOP BLOCK

2 Dadoing the front. Mount a tenoning jig, an accessory obtainable at hardware stores, in the right-hand miter slot of a table saw and clamp the drawer front in it, between wood blocks, with its inside face toward the jig and its front edge on the table. Set the height of the dado head to ½ inch, adjust the jig so that the left edge of the dado head is ½ inch from the inside face of the front, and push the jig along the miter slot to cut the dado. Reposition the drawer front to cut the dado in the opposite end.

If you do not have a tenoning jig, make a substitute of three pieces of ¾-inch stock, screwed together to form an inverted trough that slides on the rip fence (*inset*), and fasten the drawer front to this homemade jig with a C clamp. With a router, use a splining bit that cuts a groove ¼ inch wide and ½ inch deep, and follow the techniques on page 31, Step 2.

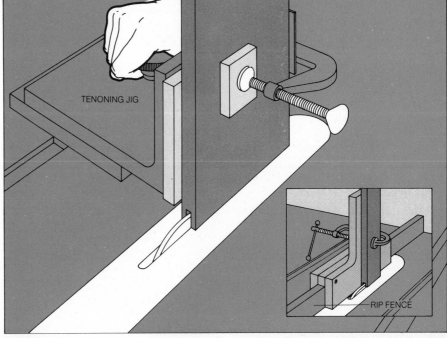

TENONING JIG

RIP FENCE

3 Trimming the double-dado tenons. Set the dado head to a height of 5/16 inch and snug the drawer front—with its inside face down—against a miter-gauge extension and a stop block positioned so that the blades will cut ¼ inch off the end of the board. To make the cut, hold the drawer front firmly with your left hand and push the miter gauge with your right. Reposition the board to trim the other end, then fit the drawer front and sides together to check the joints.

If you are using a router, set the depth at 5/16 inch and guide the tool with a clamped board.

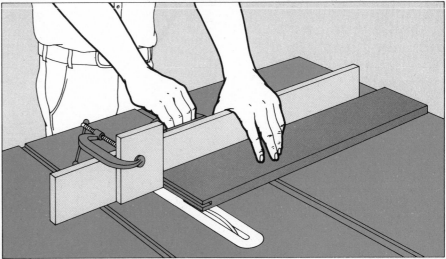

Installing Drawer Glides

1 Positioning the outer channels. For each side of a drawer opening that is not flush with the edge of the face frame, cut a plywood spacer as long as the cabinet is deep, at least 3 inches wide, and as thick as the distance inside the cabinet from the cabinet side to the edge of the face frame. Set each spacer, edge up, on a drawer support and against the cabinet side or partition, drill pilot holes for No. 8 screws 1¼ inches long, through the spacer and into the side or partition, and screw the spacer in place.

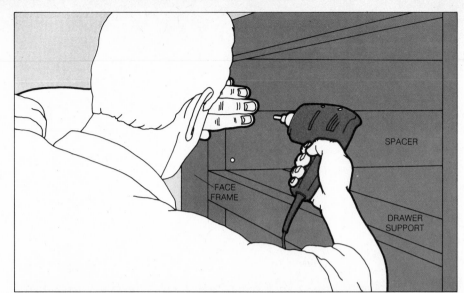

SPACER

FACE FRAME

DRAWER SUPPORT

2 Mounting the glides. Set the lower edge of each outer channel flush with the lower edge of the spacer, set the front edge of the channel flush with the front of the cabinet, and mark the locations of the channel's oblong screw holes. Drill pilot holes at the marks and fasten the channel to the spacer or cabinet with the screws provided by the manufacturer.

Screw the inner channels to the sides of the drawer (*inset*) at the positions that are called for in the manufacturer's instructions.

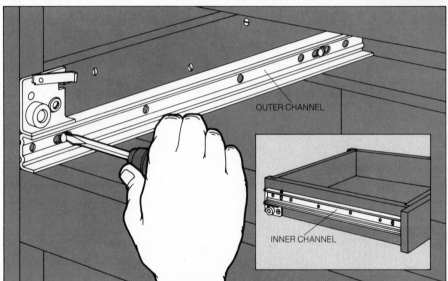

OUTER CHANNEL

INNER CHANNEL

3 Adjusting the glides. Align the inner-channel tracks with the front wheels of the outer channels and slide the drawer into the cabinet opening; if the drawer is blocked by stops in the channel, tilt its front up, then slide it the rest of the way. Check the drawer's position: It should close flush against the cabinet, with straight and equal clearances around the drawer front. If it does not, loosen the inner-channel screws and move the tracks up or down to adjust the clearances, or loosen the outer-channel screws and slide the tracks forward or back to adjust the depth of run. When the drawer fits, drill pilot holes and drive screws through the circular screw holes in the inner and outer channels.

Putting In the Doors

Choose a door that suits the use and location of the cabinet. In tight quarters, sliding doors may be preferable, because they do not open out into the space in front of a cabinet, but they have the drawback of providing access to only half the cabinet at a time. Hinged doors are more versatile and far more common. Usually installed so that they will swing on one side, they can also pivot at the top or bottom, and a door that is hinged along the bottom can double as a work surface if it is also braced by hardware such as continuous piano hinges and stay supports (page 41).

On a hinged door, as on a drawer front, a lipped or overlapping fit against the cabinet front is more suitable for built-ins than a flush fit within an opening, because overlapping doors forgive slight errors in fitting.

Ready-made cabinet doors are available at lumber mills in a variety of standard styles, but you can easily build your own. The design you choose should reflect both the quality of the cabinet and the tools at your disposal. Thus, you can simply cut a plain, flat door from high-quality plywood, or you may prefer to assemble a relatively sophisticated frame-and-panel design.

A frame-and-panel door calls for careful planning before construction: you must, for instance, add 2 inches to the length of horizontal frame pieces to allow for tenons in mortise-and-tenon joints, and subtract ¼ inch from the panel to allow for expansion and contraction. When you fit the pieces of this door together, glue only the corners of the frame and allow the panel itself to "float" in the frame. A table saw simplifies and speeds the construction of a frame-and-panel door, but you can also handle the job using only a router.

Whatever door design you choose, use the drawings and captions on pages 40-41 as a guide to the appropriate hardware. On a door with a hinged edge longer than 2 feet, install three hinges; on any door, whatever the number of the hinges, the sum of the hinge lengths should be at least one sixth the length of the hinged edge of the door.

The Classic Designs for Cabinet Doors

A plain panel door. For a simple cabinet front, cut a door from veneer-core plywood at least ¾ inch thick. To make a lipped design, as in this example, cut the door ½ inch larger than the dimensions of the opening, then cut rabbets on the back edges of the door to the size—generally ⅜ inch by ⅜ inch—of the offset of the hinges (page 40). Use a router with a quarter-round bit to round the door's exterior edges, or bevel the edges back at a 30° angle (inset).

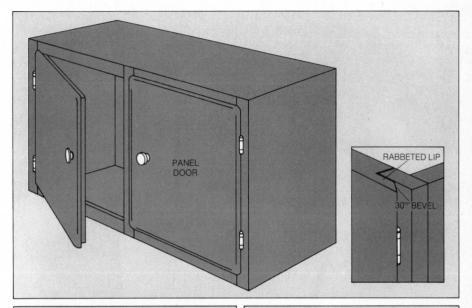

PANEL DOOR

RABBETED LIP
30° BEVEL

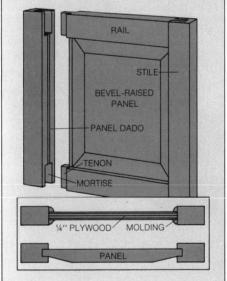

RAIL
STILE
BEVEL-RAISED PANEL
PANEL DADO
TENON
MORTISE

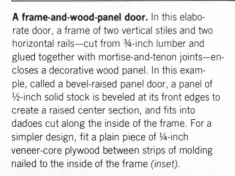

¼" PLYWOOD   MOLDING
PANEL

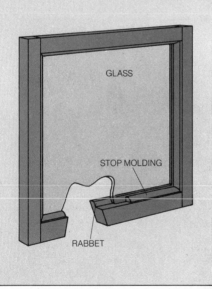

GLASS
STOP MOLDING
RABBET

A frame-and-wood-panel door. In this elaborate door, a frame of two vertical stiles and two horizontal rails—cut from ¾-inch lumber and glued together with mortise-and-tenon joints—encloses a decorative wood panel. In this example, called a bevel-raised panel door, a panel of ½-inch solid stock is beveled at its front edges to create a raised center section, and fits into dadoes cut along the inside of the frame. For a simpler design, fit a plain piece of ¼-inch veneer-core plywood between strips of molding nailed to the inside of the frame (inset).

A frame-and-glass door. For a door with a panel of glass—or of cane, metal mesh or cloth—cut mortise-and-tenon joints (pages 38-39), assemble and glue the frame, and then cut rabbets ½ inch deep and ⅜ inch wide around its back edges. Secure the material in the rabbets with lengths of molding nailed to the outer edges of the rabbets; the width of the molding is determined by the thickness of the panel.

Making the Frame
for a Paneled Door

1 **Dadoing the frame pieces.** To cut grooves on a table saw (*left*) fit it with a ¼-inch dado head (*page 24*), set the rip fence ½ inch from the outer blade, and clamp an auxiliary fence—a 2-by-4 nailed to a piece of plywood—on the other side of the blade. Raise the dado head to a height of ¼ inch, set a frame piece of ¾-inch solid stock firmly in place, its inside edge down and its outside face against the rip fence, and hold the auxiliary fence against it with your left hand. Feed the entire piece across the blades with your right hand. Similarly dado the other pieces, always with the outside face against the rip fence.

To cut these dadoes with a router (*right*), clamp a frame piece, inside edge up, between scrap pieces and nail stop blocks to the worktable at the sides and the right end of the assembly to steady the work. Fit the router with a ³⁄₁₆-inch bit set to a cutting depth of ¼ inch, and use a router jig to guide the bit ¼ inch in from the edge of the frame piece. Cut the dado, then turn the jig around and make a second pass with the router on the opposite side.

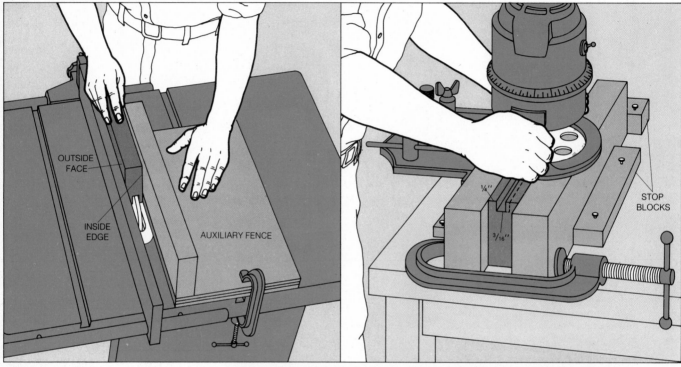

OUTSIDE FACE

INSIDE EDGE

AUXILIARY FENCE

¼"

³⁄₁₆"

STOP BLOCKS

2 **Mortising the stiles.** To cut the mortises on a table saw, reset the dado head to 1¹⁄₁₆ inches, position each stile piece as in Step 1, above, but omit the auxiliary fence; move each piece a short distance against the blades. Then remove the stile to measure the straight section of the mortise (the dado head cuts a mortise round at one end; do not include the rounded end when measuring). When the straight section equals the width of the rail less ¼ inch, mark the fence at the end of the stile as a stopping point when you feed the wood for the remaining mortises.

To cut the mortises with a router, follow the techniques for dadoing but make repeated passes, increasing the cutting depth of the bit by maximum increments of ⅜ inch, until you have deepened the cuts to 1¹⁄₁₆ inches at the stile ends.

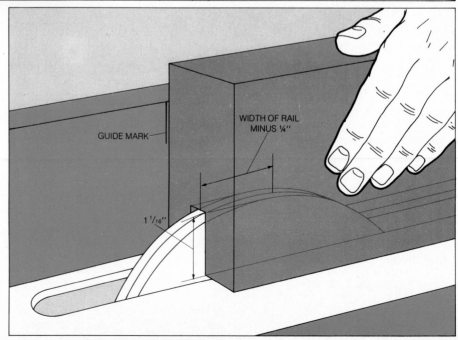

GUIDE MARK

WIDTH OF RAIL MINUS ¼"

1¹⁄₁₆"

3 Cutting tenons on the rails. If you are using a table saw *(left)*, fit it with an ordinary blade set to a cutting depth of ¼ inch. Use the miter gauge *(page 14)* to cut across both faces of a rail along marked lines—called shoulder lines—1 inch in from each end. To complete the tenons *(right)*, secure the rail vertically in a commercial or homemade tenoning jig *(page 35, Step 2)*, adjust the jig for a cut ¼ inch in from the outer face of the rail, set the blade height to 1 inch and run the rail across the blade for a "cheek" cut. Turn the rail around to cut a second cheek, completing the tenon.

To make tenons with a router, cut rabbets ¼ inch deep and 1 inch wide *(pages 22-23)*.

When all the frame pieces are shaped, test-assemble them and sand or chisel them as necessary for a perfect fit. Cut a plywood or hardboard panel ¼ inch smaller on each side than the distance between the bottoms of the dadoes on opposite sides, beveling the panel if desired as explained below. Assemble panel and frame, gluing only the mortise-and-tenon joints.

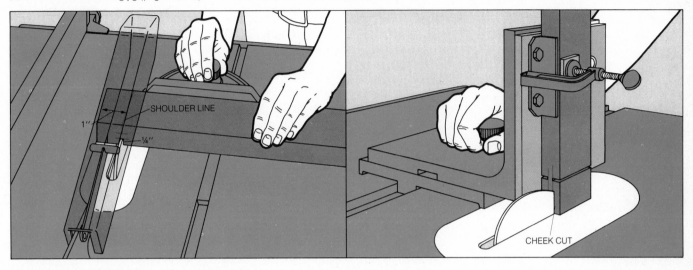

SHOULDER LINE
1″
¼″
CHEEK CUT

Beveling the Panel

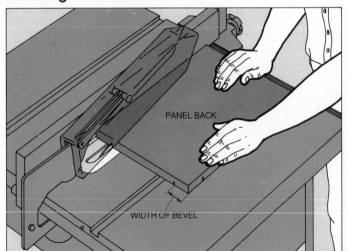

PANEL BACK
WIDTH OF BEVEL

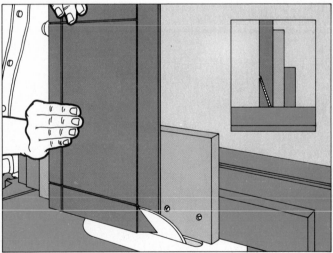

1 Starting the bevel. When using a table saw, set the blade to a cutting depth of $^{1}/_{16}$ inch and position the rip fence so that the distance between it and the blade equals the width of the panel bevel—generally about 2 inches. Hold the panel face down, with one edge flush against the rip fence, and cut along its face; repeat these cuts on the other three edges.

If you do not have a table saw, use a circular saw with its blade at a depth of $^{1}/_{16}$ inch; clamp a guide to the panel to make a straight cut.

2 Cutting the bevel. Move the rip fence of the table saw to the left of the blade and secure a tall auxiliary fence to it *(page 24, Step 4)*. Holding the panel with its back against the fence and its edge along the blade, adjust the fence position, blade projection and blade tilt for a cut like that in the inset. The blade should enter the edge $^{3}/_{16}$ inch from the panel back and emerge from the front just below the cut made in Step 2. Keeping both hands well above the blade, slide the panel along the fence to cut the bevels around all four edges, then sand them smooth.

If you use a router, fit it with a beveling bit and cut sharp 30° bevels on the panel edges.

Hardware for Hinged Doors

A butt hinge. For doors that have frames of solid lumber, the most commonly used hinge resembles those used on house doors, and consists of two rectangular leaves that pivot on a central pin. (Hinges for other doors and special situations are shown on these two pages.) In the example at near right, the leaves of a butt hinge are recessed, or mortised, into the face frame of the cabinet and the edge of a flush door; at far right, the leaves are surface-mounted —that is, installed without mortises—on the side of the cabinet and the edge of an overlapping door. Use loose-pin butt hinges, which permit you to pull out the pin and remove the door without having to unscrew the leaves.

An offset hinge. For cabinets made entirely of plywood—which does not securely hold screws set into its edges, required with butt hinges— offset, or shutter, hinges permit fastening to the plywood surfaces, as in this overlapping door. All offset hinges have to be mortised rather than surface-mounted; the offset leaf comes in various sizes to match standard plywood thicknesses.

A semiconcealed hinge. Designed for lipped (rabbeted) and for partially overlapping doors, this hinge has one leaf surface-mounted on the face of the cabinet and an offset leaf mortised into the back of the door. For the overlapping door in this example, the door leaf has an offset like that of a shutter hinge; on a lipped door (*inset*) the hinge has a double offset. Buy the hinges for a lipped door before rabbeting the door, then rabbet the lip to a depth that exactly matches the offset of the hinge.

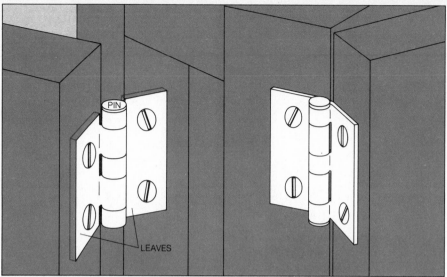

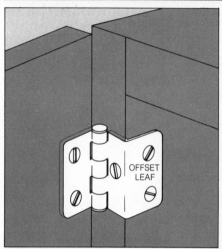

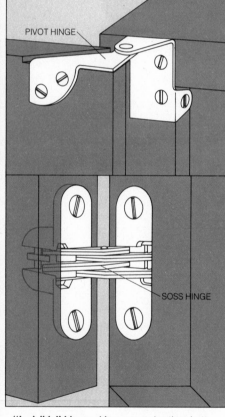

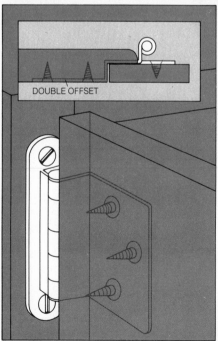

"Invisible" hinges. More expensive than butt hinges and trickier to install, pivot hinges (*above, top*) and patented Soss hinges (*above, bottom*) are fitted to doors in a way that makes the hinge nearly or completely invisible. Pivot hinges are installed in slanting mortises at the top and bottom edges of a door; when the door is closed, only a bit of the pivot is visible from the front. Soss hinges, which resemble sets of interlocking knife blades, are fitted into deep mortises in a flush door and in the cabinet; these hinges are invisible when the door is closed.

Hardware for extra support. On a very heavy door, and on a door subjected to special strain when opened, use a continuous, or piano, hinge—essentially a surface-mounted butt hinge that runs the entire length of the door. In this example a door drops down to become a work surface; the open, cantilevered door would be too bouncy without the folding stay supports screwed to the side of the cabinet and the back of the door to provide reinforcement and stability. Stay supports can also be used to control the swing of a conventional door.

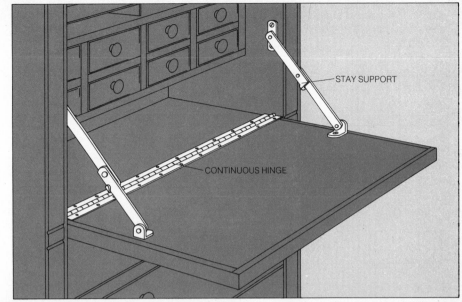

STAY SUPPORT

CONTINUOUS HINGE

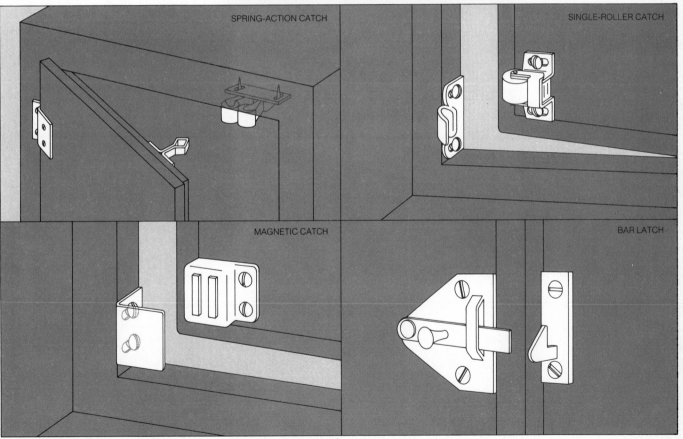

SPRING-ACTION CATCH

SINGLE-ROLLER CATCH

MAGNETIC CATCH

BAR LATCH

Catches and latches. Each of these pieces of hardware has a characteristic method of installation and special advantages and disadvantages. A spring-action catch (*top left*) calls for the alignment of an arrow-shaped strike, mounted on the door, with spring-loaded double rollers mounted inside the cabinet; the assembly is especially durable and relatively quiet. On a single-roller catch (*top right*), the roller is on the door and fits into a strike plate mounted on the cabinet; this catch is very quiet because it holds the closed door slightly away from the cabinet. In a magnetic catch (*bottom left*) the parts need not align exactly, but the catch is noisy and the magnet weakens with age. An alternative to all of these concealed catches is exterior hardware, such as a bar latch (*bottom right*); this latch serves as a door pull as well as a catch.

Tough, Long-lasting Finishes for Built-ins

Built-ins can be finished like conventional furniture, with oils, lacquer, shellac or wax, but they generally get harder use and require more durable finishing.

In the kitchen, a finish must resist stains from spilled food, and countertops must take the scorching heat of cookware just off the stove; in bathrooms, the finish is exposed to steam and constant moisture, and throughout the house built-in surfaces must resist abrasion, chipping and scratching. Coatings and countertops particularly suited to such heavy-duty use are described in the charts below and at right.

Because most built-ins combine plywood with solid lumber, special care is necessary in matching the finishes. Fill nicks and nail holes with wood putty (matching the color of the wood if you will use a clear finish). Sand surfaces with 80-grit sandpaper, and follow up with a light sanding with 120-grit. Open-grained veneers, such as oak or walnut, must be filled with paste wood-grain filler and resanded; closed-grained hardwoods such as birch need not be filled.

Plywood edges are a particular problem. Unless they are covered by edging (page 12, Step 6) or veneer tape, the edges need to be filled with wood putty and sanded smooth. And if for economy you use fir plywood—much cheaper than even the least expensive veneered plywood—you will have difficulty with its prominent "wild" grain pattern, which shows through even several coats of paint in a way that most people find unattractive. The fir grain can be tamed, but seldom entirely concealed, with sealer especially made for this purpose, such as Danish Wood Finish and Pre-Sealer.

Countertop surfaces generally are applied after the cabinet is installed. For some surfaces you must prepare the countertop in advance. Plastic laminate, the most common, requires a built-up edge on an unfinished plywood countertop (page 29, Step 1, inset).

Marble or slate countertops, generally from ¾ to ⅞ inch thick, are more elegant—and more expensive. In these thicknesses, stone does not need a specially prepared countertop; a commercial dealer (listed under "Marble" or "Monuments" in the Yellow Pages) will cut each piece to your specifications.

If you use ⅜-inch slate rather than the more expensive ¾-inch material, install a plywood countertop and cover its exposed edges with 1⅛-inch hardwood nosing (page 29, Step 2), set flush with the bottom of the countertop and protruding above the top.

Stone countertops are heavy—as much as 20 pounds per running foot—and fragile; recruit helpers to support the slab at 3-foot intervals, to prevent the stone from breaking of its own weight.

A Range of Coatings

Material	Characteristics	Limitations	Comments
Enamel, oil-based	Toughest of all coatings; resists moisture and stains; opaque, available in all colors; hides imperfections in wood and construction	Primer must be used; disagreeable fumes from solvent when wet	High-gloss type is most durable. Recommended for use on less expensive woods with unattractive grain
Stain, oil-based	Lightens or darkens wood; must be covered by varnish; easier to use than water-based stains (below)	Tones down pattern of grain; does not give color range achievable with water-based stains	Good choice for clear-finished cabinets if color is satisfactory
Stain, water-based	Sold as a powder that is mixed with water; penetrates wood deeply and is available in all colors; must be covered with a clear finish	Somewhat difficult to mix; raises the grain of the wood so that surface must be sanded repeatedly	A frequent choice, despite difficulties of use, because of its color qualities
Varnish, spar	Clear, oil-based finish, applied in two coats (first coat must be thinned with turpentine); weather-resistant, particularly to salt air	Too soft for indoor applications; must be recoated often	Good choice for clear-finished outdoor built-ins
Varnish, urethane	Clear finish; applied in at least two coats (sand between coats); excellent durability and abrasion-resistance; very resistant to moisture and stains	Although exterior grade is available, it generally is not considered as weather-resistant as spar varnish (above)	Also known as polyurethane; aliphatic type discolors least and high-gloss is most durable; recommended for clear-finished interior built-ins

Choosing a wood finish. The paints, stains and varnishes best suited for finishing the wood of built-ins are described in this chart. All are quite tough, and some, such as urethane varnish and high-quality oil-based enamel, can substitute for countertops if great resistance to moisture and cleaning compounds is not essential. Latex paints are not listed because of their limited durability, but they can be used where they will not be exposed to heavy use.

Countertop Surfaces

Material	Characteristics	Limitations	Comments
SYNTHETICS			
Plastic laminate	Inexpensive and available in a wide range of glossy colors, patterns and textures, including imitation marble, slate and wood grain; also a special, costly type made with genuine wood veneer; pieces are cut to size from 4-by-8 sheets with a scoring tool and fastened with adhesive; edges are finished with a router; exceptionally tough, resisting water and most stains	Edges can chip and surface can scratch; sheets peel away if water seeps beneath them; scorched by cigarettes and very hot cooking pots	Most commonly used countertop; recommended for all applications where appearance is satisfactory
Ceramic tile	Beautifully smooth and shiny surface; heat resistant; available in many colors; installed in mastic and secured with grout; ordinarily ¼ inch thick, in square or hexagonal shapes 1 to 12 inches across; almost totally water- and heat-resistant	Can chip, scratch or crack; grout between tiles stains easily; hard surface makes kitchenware clatter and can cause breakage	Stains can be removed with diluted bleach; not the most practical surface for kitchens or bathrooms
Cultured marble	Made of marble chips embedded in plastic; looks like marble and has similar colors but is water- and stain-resistant and much stronger. Ordinarily ¾ inch thick	Must be cut by a professional; on some types, marble chips form a surface layer only, making it impossible to repair scratches and scorches; not heat-resistant	Only the type containing marble mixed through is recommended
Acrylic-resin sheets ("synthetic marble")	Often called Corian, a trade name; available in olive and off-white, with marbling streaks; looks much like marble; can be cut with a power saw and shaped with a router; resists moisture, heat, stains and cracks. Ordinarily ¾ inch thick	Limited range of colors; scratches easily; costly	Scratches and scorches can be sanded out
STONES			
Granite	Strong and impervious to heat, moisture and stains; takes a bright polish; available in mottled shades of gray, pink, red, black and blue; ordinarily ⅞ inch thick	Twice as expensive as other stones; very heavy; hard	
Marble	Porous and brittle; available in a wide range of colors and patterns; takes a bright polish; ordinarily ¾ inch thick	Scratches, cracks and breaks easily; is easily stained—even by water	Wax sealer can be used to improve stain resistance; professionals can sometimes repair cracks and scratches; especially suitable for formal rooms
Slate	Heat-resistant; relatively inexpensive; available in black, red, gray and gray-green. Ordinarily ⅜ or ¾ inch thick	Cracks and scratches easily; will not take a bright polish; very brittle	Often used as a thin ⅜-inch veneer over a hidden plywood top (pages 42, 45)

Choosing a countertop. The headings of this chart are identical with those of the chart on the opposite page, but the materials in the first column are grouped in two categories: a group of countertops made of natural stone, and a second group consisting of synthetic countertops and countertop surfaces. All these materials offer a variety of textures and colors that add elegance to a built-in and to the room it fits into. All provide much greater resistance to moisture, heat and stains than finished wood, and they are used not only to top kitchen cabinets, bathroom counters and bars but also for parts of shelves and bookcases that might be resting places for ashtrays or drink glasses.

Installing a
Solid-Stone Countertop

1 **Applying adhesive.** With a caulking gun apply 1-inch beads of neoprene adhesive to the plywood strips at the top of the carcass, running the beads about 1½ inches from the front and back edges. Wipe the bottom side of the stone slab clean and, with one helper for every 3 feet of stone, lift it over the cabinet. Set the back edge on the cabinet, tight against the wall, then slowly lower the front edge onto the frame.

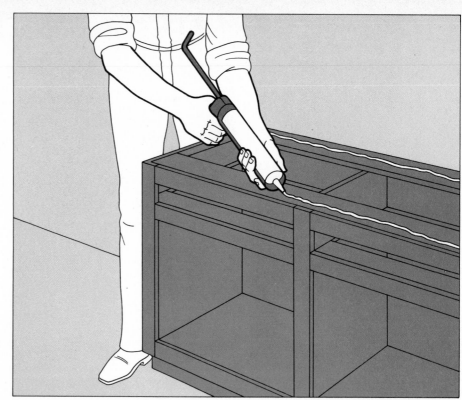

2 **Adjusting the overhang.** Hold a wood block 1 inch thick flat against the carcass just beneath the stone top, and use the block as a gauge to check the overhang of the stone top. Have a helper adjust the top by pushing it until the overhang is even on all exposed sides; wipe off any excess adhesive immediately with a wet rag.

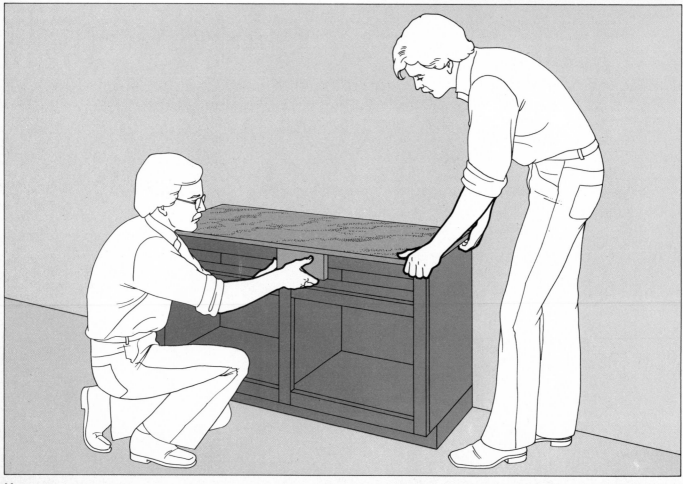

Setting a Slate Slab on a Wooden Countertop

1 **Preparing the countertop.** In a countertop edged with 1⅛-inch nosing *(page 29, Step 2)*, saw four access holes, each about 6 inches square, by drilling holes at the corners and cutting out the squares with a saber saw. Locate them about 8 inches from the front of the cabinet and space them to avoid any cabinet partitions.

2 **Lowering the stone.** After applying adhesive to the edges of the countertop, lay three or four scraps of wood across the countertop nosing, resting their inner ends on the countertop, and assemble at least two helpers to assist you in handling the stone. With one worker at each end of the cabinet and the third reaching up through one pair of access holes, gently lower the stone veneer onto the countertop, resting the front edge of the veneer on the scrap wood pieces. Slide the veneer tight against the walls at the back or side of the cabinet. Now have two helpers raise the veneer slightly through the access holes while you remove the wood scraps; finally, have the helpers at the access holes gently lower the veneer to the countertop.

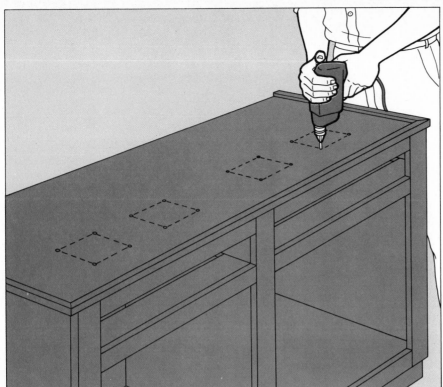

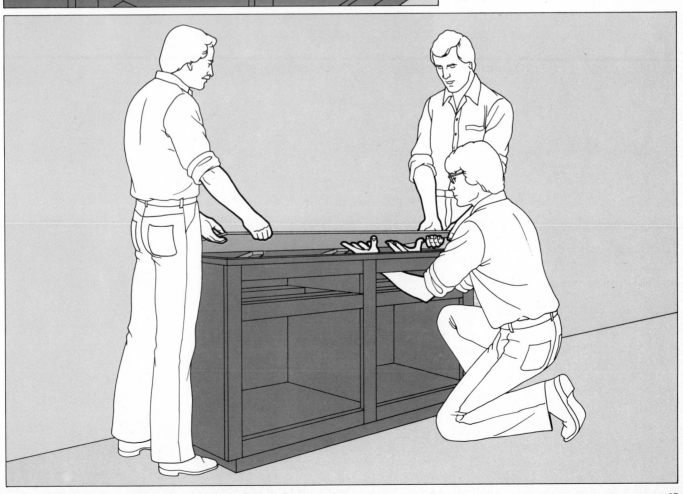

Anchoring a Cabinet to the Frame of the House

Like any other built-in, a cabinet must be fastened to a house. Cabinets that hang on walls are fastened to the studs within the walls; ceiling cabinets hang from the joists above the ceilings. Even floor cabinets are fastened to the subflooring and, if they stand against a wall, to studs.

Obviously, locating studs and joists is the first step in installing a cabinet. Drill ⅛-inch holes just above a baseboard and probe behind the wall with a length of stiff wire to locate two studs and determine their spacing; remove tiles or ceiling board to determine the location and direction of two ceiling joists.

Mark off the cabinet location by drawing lines on the wall or ceiling or, to avoid marring paint or paneling, by running strips of masking tape. For a wall cabinet, you will need a horizontal line for the bottom of the cabinet (this line is normally 5 feet above the floor) and a vertical line for one side. Mark the center of each stud below the bottom of the installation area and above the top.

For ceiling cabinets, use the hanging frame (page 55, middle) as a template to outline the installation area, then mark the joist centers; for floor cabinets, use the base frame. Floor cabinets can be installed right over any flooring; if the room is carpeted, set the base frame in place, cut the carpeting along the edges of the frame with a utility knife, then remove that section of the carpeting.

Placing a cabinet in a wall recess is trickier. Because walls and ceilings are rarely completely flat, a wall cabinet should be about ¼ inch narrower than the recess; the gaps between the cabinet and the flanking walls can be covered with molding. A cabinet that rises to the ceiling should be set about ½ inch below the ceiling. To allow for the molding that will cover the gap between the cabinet and the ceiling, build a cabinet so that its front will be set back at least 2 inches from the front corners of the recess.

For the installation job itself, you must nail a horizontal 1-by-3 to the wall as a temporary ledger (below) to support a wall cabinet and keep it level during the job. For a heavy cabinet or a set of cabinets, place vertical 2-by-4 props between the cabinet bottom and the floor. Remove the baseboard before installing a base cabinet; later on, cut it so that it will fit against the edges of the installed cabinet. If the hinges of the cabinet doors have removable pins, take the doors off before starting the job. And recruit enough helpers to hold cabinets steady as you drill pilot holes and drive screws.

The best fasteners are flat-head screws long enough to run at least 1 inch into the supporting studs or joists; use No. 8 screws and finish washers, available at hardware stores. In masonry walls use ex-

panding shields that fit into drilled holes in the wall, and machine bolts that screw through the cabinet and into the shields. Secure cabinets to the wall at top and bottom. The wall cabinets in this chapter are built with hanging bars (page 16), which strengthen a unit at the top, where it is most apt to pull away from the wall.

On a plaster wall, you can sand away the small bumps that prevent a cabinet from fitting snugly and hanging plumb, but for larger wall irregularities—particularly in wallboard—it is easier to alter the cabinet. A well-built cabinet has a face frame and ½-inch scribing strips (page 16); the frame and strips can be planed to fit against most bumps and depressions. The strips protrude past the back of a cabinet, creating a gap between the back panel and the wall; use shingle shims to fill this gap and to plumb a cabinet.

To complete an installation, cover the gaps between the cabinet and the wall and ceiling. Many molding styles are available; in the examples on these pages a right-angled cove molding is used to cover a gap of up to ½ inch between a cabinet and a wall; a 2-inch cornice molding covers a similar gap between a cabinet top and a ceiling. To cover a larger gap—as much as 6 inches—between a cabinet and the ceiling, use a soffit made of plywood, of wood matching the cabinet, or of painted or papered wallboard.

Hanging a Wall Cabinet

1 **Installing a temporary ledger.** Set a 1-by-3 cut to the width of the cabinet flat against the wall, with its top at the line that marks the cabinet bottom, and nail the board to each stud it crosses; let the nailheads protrude ¼ inch. Check the board to be sure it is level; if it is not, remove enough nails to reset it.

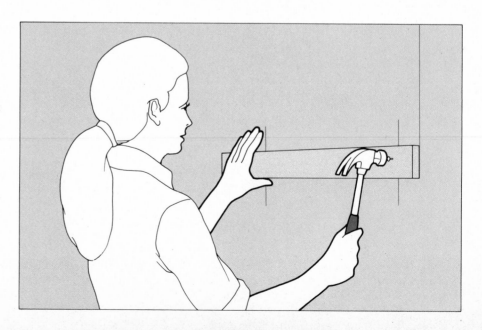

2 **Shimming the top of the cabinet.** Set the back of the cabinet on the ledger and align the side with the vertical mark you have made on the wall, then have a helper hold the cabinet against the wall while you use a level to check the face for plumb. If the top of the cabinet must move out from the wall, insert a shim at each stud and tap it down far enough to move the cabinet top the required distance. If the cabinet must move out at the bottom, use shims at the top only to fill the gap between the back and the wall; tap them into place without moving the cabinet.

In a wall recess where you cannot reach over the top of a cabinet to insert shims, nail a ¾-inch wood strip to the top of the cabinet back between the scribing strips, and shim the bottom of the cabinet (*Step 3, below*) to make it plumb. In either case, proceed immediately to Step 3.

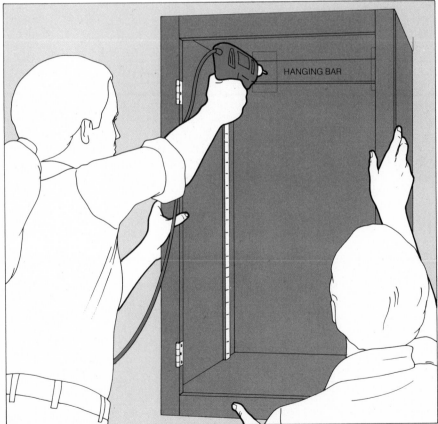

HANGING BAR

Hiding Gaps with Molding

3 **Fastening the cabinet to the wall.** Drill pilot holes through the hanging bar, cabinet back and shims, and into the studs; then screw the top of the cabinet to the wall with 3-inch No. 8 screws. Remove the ledger and shim the cabinet bottom at each stud, filling the gap between the back and the wall and, if neces-

sary, plumbing the cabinet. While your helper presses the cabinet against the bottom shims, drill and drive screws through the cabinet back and through these shims into the studs.

Trim the protruding shim ends with a handsaw: cut almost to the wall, then snap off the waste.

At the sides of a cabinet. Cut two strips of ¾-inch cove molding to the height of the cabinet and cut the bottom end of each strip to a line that reverses the contour of the molding (*inset*). Set the flat sides of the moldings in the angle formed by the cabinet and the wall and fasten the strip to the cabinet with brads spaced 6 inches apart.

Around a recessed wall cabinet. Cut a strip of 2-inch cornice molding to the width of the recess, hold it in place against the ceiling and the face of the cabinet and trace its bottom edge across the cabinet; then nail a 1-by-¾-inch nailing strip of the same length flat against the cabinet, with its bottom at the traced line. Set the bottom of the molding flush with the bottom of the nailing strip and nail the molding to the strip.

Cut a strip of ¾-inch cove molding to the width of the recess, miter the ends to a 45° angle and nail the molding to the cabinet directly beneath the nailing strip. Cut two strips of cove molding to match the height of the cabinet; miter the top of each strip to fit the top strip and cut the bottom of each by the method shown on page 47, bottom right; nail the strips to the sides of the cabinet face frame *(inset)*.

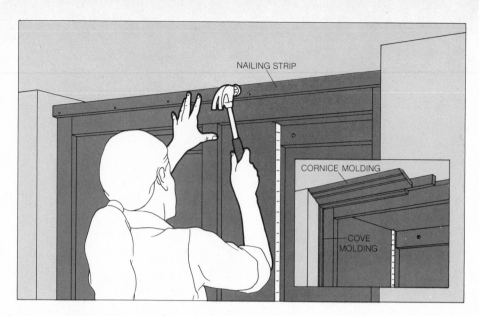

Scribing and Shaping for a Perfect Fit

Marking the scribing strips. Run masking tape along the outside of each scribing strip, have a helper hold the cabinet on a temporary ledger and shim the back to make the cabinet plumb *(page 47, Step 2)*; if the cabinet must be shimmed at the bottom, use props *(page 49, Step 2)* rather than a ledger to help support the cabinet. Set the legs of a compass or a pair of carpenter's dividers ¼ inch apart, place the pivot point against the wall and put the pencil at the top of a scribing strip; run the dividers down the wall. Plane each strip down to the penciled line. It may be necessary to set the cabinet back in position, then take it down and plane it several times for a precise fit.

Remove the tapes and hang the cabinet *(page 47, Step 3)*, shimming at the studs to fill gaps between the cabinet and the wall.

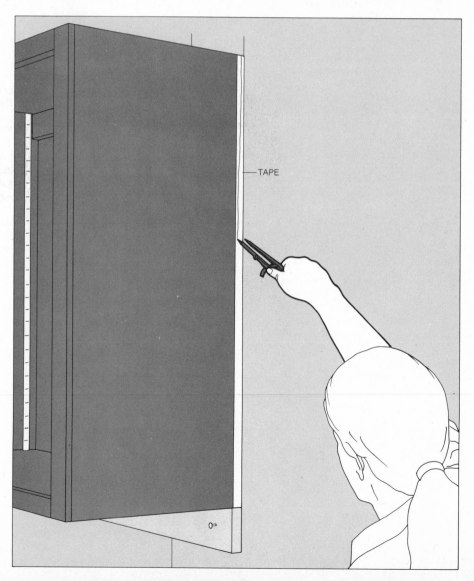

Hanging a Set of Cabinets

1 **Linking the cabinets together.** Set the cabinets side by side on the floor, face up, and clamp adjacent sides together with C clamps; protect the cabinets with scraps of soft wood between the jaws of each clamp. Drill pilot holes about 4 inches from the top and bottom and 3 inches in from the front and back, and screw the cabinets together with 1¼-inch No. 6 screws.

If the face frames will be overlapped by doors, drill pilot holes level with the fastening screws, from the inside edge of each frame into the adjacent frame and drive 3¼-inch screws into the holes. Finally, sand all the face frames to make them completely flush with each other.

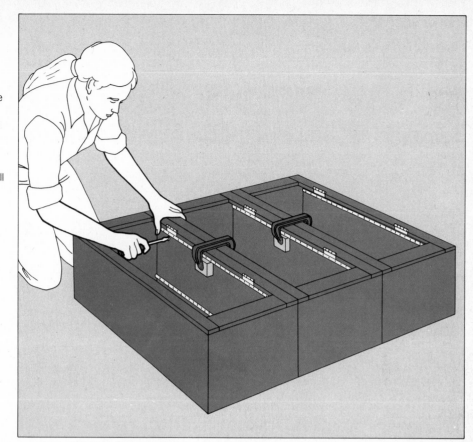

2 **Propping the cabinets against the wall.** Install a temporary ledger (*page 46, Step 1*) for the row of cabinets and, with two or more helpers, raise the cabinets onto the ledger; for additional support, position 2-by-4 props at the sides and middle of the cabinet row. Have the helpers hold the cabinets while you plumb and hang the entire set as a single unit.

A Soffit for a Ceiling Gap

1 Marking the ceiling. At 5-inch intervals, set the edge of a ruler against the sides and the face frames with the end of the ruler touching the ceiling, and mark the ceiling at the back edge of the ruler. Connect the marks with solid lines, then cut out a small section of ceiling within the lines to determine the location and direction of the joists. If the joists are perpendicular to the cabinet faces, as in the example shown here, mark the location of each joist on the line above the front of the cabinets. If they are parallel to the cabinets and there is no joist directly above the line, proceed directly to Step 2, below.

2 Installing the cleats. Cut a 1-by-2 cleat to the length of the front line on the ceiling and side cleats to fit between the front cleat and the wall, and fasten the cleats to the ceiling with their front edges directly within the lines. If the joists are perpendicular to the cabinets, nail the front cleat to each joist it crosses. If there is no joist directly above a front or side cleat, use toggle bolts (*inset*) to fasten the cleat directly to the ceiling.

Drill holes through the cleats and the ceiling board at 6-inch intervals, run the bolts through the holes in the cleat, screw the toggles onto the bolts and push the toggles through the holes in the ceiling. As you tighten each bolt, the toggles will pull the cleat to the ceiling.

Cut soffit boards long enough to cover the gaps above the cabinets and wide enough to over-lap the face frames and sides by ½ inch. Cut 45° bevels on the ends that will form corners.

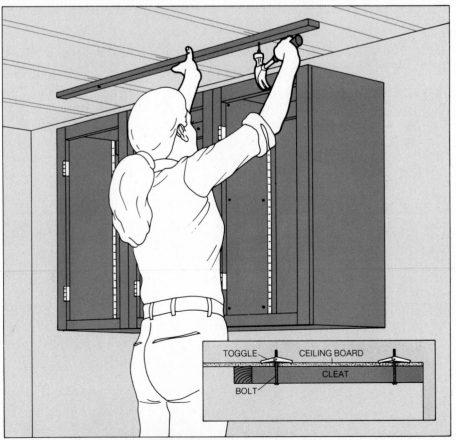

3 Fastening the soffit. At 6-inch intervals, nail the bottoms of the soffit boards to the cabinets and the tops to the cleats. At each corner, fasten the boards together with a single brad.

If a cleat is fastened to the ceiling with toggle bolts rather than nails, drill pilot holes and fasten the soffit board to the cleat with ½-inch No. 8 screws—the force of a hammer blow could rip the toggle-bolted cleat off the ceiling.

4 Covering the ceiling joint. Set a strip of cornice molding against the ceiling and the front soffit board, and mark the bottom edge of the molding at the ends of the board; mark the side moldings to fit between the front of the soffit and the wall. For each corner, place the moldings upside down in a miter box, with the angled surfaces against the fence and bottom of the box. Set the saw to a 45° angle and cut the piece for the left side of the corner with the saw handle at the left (*inset*), the piece for the right side with the handle at the right. Nail the moldings to the soffit boards at 6-inch intervals.

LEFT SIDE OF CORNER

5 Covering the cabinet joint. Cut strips of ¾-inch cove molding to the length and width of the cabinets and make 45° miter cuts at the ends that will form exterior corners; then set each strip flush with the bottom edge of a soffit board and nail the strip to the cabinet at 6-inch intervals.

If your soffit consists of wallboard covered with wallpaper, choose a cove molding slightly wider than the bottom edge of the soffit, to conceal the exposed edge of the wallpaper.

Mounting a Base Cabinet

1 **Leveling the base.** Set the base in position and tap shims under one or more corners to level it; tap additional shims at the front of the base under each spreader to fill any gaps between the base and floor. For a base that stands against a wall, mark the positions of studs along its rear edge and at the height of the cabinet top.

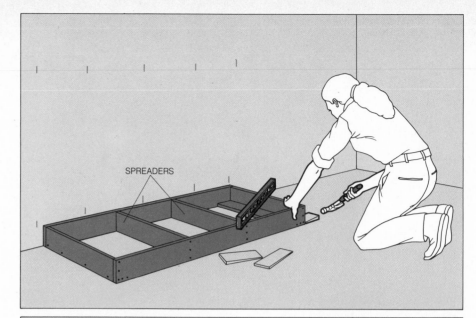

2 **Fastening the base.** At each corner of the base, drill a pilot hole and drive a 2½-inch No. 8 screw through the screwing strip, the shim, the floor and the subfloor. At each spreader, toe-nail through the base, shim and floor. Trim the ends of the shims *(page 47, Step 3).*

An island-cabinet base *(inset)* has extra 1-by-4 screwing strips at the bottom and 1-by-2 strips at the top: screw the base down at three points along each bottom strip, and mark the base front at the center of each top strip.

Cover the exposed sides of the base and shims with vinyl cove molding or ¼-inch plywood boards cut ¼ inch wider than the base sides and scribed and planed so that the bottom edge fits the floor and the top edge rests about ¼ inch below the top of the base side. Fasten the plywood with 1-inch brads.

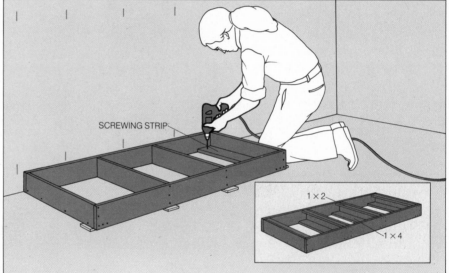

3 **Fastening the cabinet to the base.** Set the cabinet with its back against the wall and its sides and front overlapping the base frame by 3 inches; inside the cabinet measure 3 inches in from each side and drive fourpenny finishing nails at 6-inch intervals through the cabinet bottom into the sides of the frame.

On an island cabinet, use ¾-inch No. 8 screws rather than nails and fasten the bottom at three points along each top screwing strip, lining the screws up with the marks made at the top of the base front in Step 2.

4 **Screwing a cabinet to the wall.** At each stud position, tap a shim between the wall and the cabinet back to fill any gap, then drill a pilot hole and drive a 2¼-inch No. 8 screw through the cabinet back, the shims and the wall, and into the stud. Trim the protruding shim ends.

Fitting a Cabinet Top to an Alcove

1 **Making a template.** Cut two pieces of ¼-inch plywood, each 6 inches longer than half the width of the alcove and wide enough to overhang the front of the cabinet by 2 inches. Set the pieces on the cabinet, push them into the corners and, using carpenter's dividers with the legs set slightly wider than the widest gap between the wall and the plywood, scribe the contours of the side and back walls on both pieces of plywood. Remove the plywood, and plane or saw the edges of both pieces to the pencil lines. Replace both halves of the template against the corners of the alcove and tack them together at their overlap. Across the front of the template, draw a guideline 1 inch out from the front of the cabinet frame.

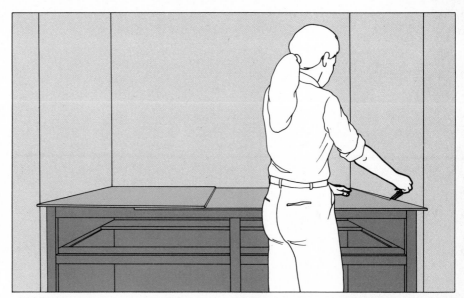

2 **Marking the cabinet top.** Remove the template from the cabinet and clamp it to the finished side of the cabinet top, with the guideline on the template flush with the front of the top, and outline the template edges on the top. Remove the template and cut the edges of the cabinet top with a handsaw, then plane them smooth.

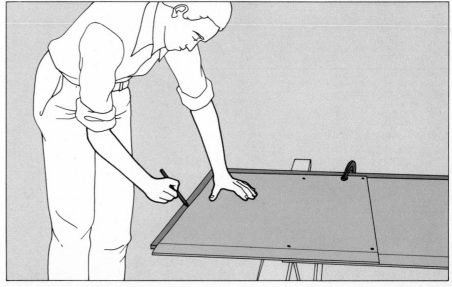

3 **Fastening the cabinet top.** Set the cabinet top in place flush with the alcove walls, drill pilot holes up through the cabinet screwing strips and drive 1¼-inch No. 8 screws into the top at 6-inch intervals. Cover the exposed edge of the cabinet top with edging (page 12).

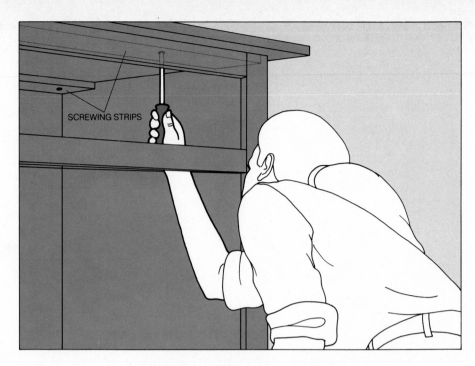

SCREWING STRIPS

Stacking a Two-Piece Unit

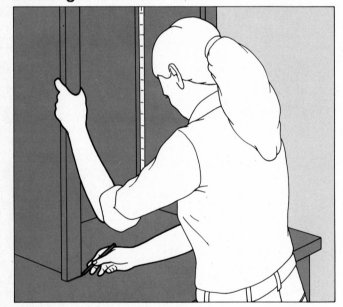

A bookcase on a base cabinet. Set in place the upper half of the unit—in this example, a bookcase assembled with hanging bars but without a base (page 18)—and outline the bottoms of the stiles on the cabinet top. Remove the bookcase, drill a pilot hole down through the cabinet top at the center of each stile position, then replace the bookcase and drive 2-inch No. 8 screws up through the top into each stile. Shim the back of the bookcase at the position of each stud (page 47, Step 2), drill pilot holes through the hanging bars and screw the bookcase to the studs. Nail cornice molding directly to the face frame to conceal the gaps between the top of the unit and the ceiling.

Installing a Floor-to-Ceiling Unit

1 **Raising the unit.** After installing a base (page 52, Steps 1 and 2), set the unit—here, a bookcase—face down on the floor and, with a helper, swing it upward on its lower front edge until it stands upright in front of the base.

2 **Fastening the unit in place.** With a helper, set the unit on the base and against the wall, with front and sides overlapping the base by 3 inches. Nail the unit bottom to the base *(page 52, Step 3)*, then shim the top and drive screws through the hanging bar into the studs. Use cornice molding *(page 51, Steps 4-5)* to hide the gaps between the unit top and the ceiling.

For a unit installed as a room divider, with one side against a wall, build a base with extra screwing strips *(page 52, Step 2, inset)*. Use the same base for a unit that has no wall support, and fasten the unit to the ceiling joists. Install a ¾-inch plywood filler strip, shimmed flush with the ceiling, between the unit and the ceiling, and drive 3½-inch No. 10 screws through the unit top and the filler strip into the joist or joists above. If the joists run parallel to the unit, drive the screws every 16 inches along one joist; otherwise drive the screws into every joist that crosses it.

Hanging Cabinets from the Ceiling

1 **A hanging frame for a ceiling unit.** The outside of this frame consists of ¾-inch plywood boards 6 inches wide, cut to the length and width of the cabinets that will hang from it and butt-nailed at the corners. Upper and lower crosspieces are butt-nailed in place through the outside of the frame. The upper crosspieces are 2-by-4s spaced at equal intervals and set perpendicular to the overhead joists; they are shimmed at the joist positions to make the frame level and fastened to the joists with 3½-inch No. 10 screws. The lower crosspieces—2-by-4s at front and back, a 2-by-6 in the middle—are positioned over the hanging bars *(Step 2, below)*.

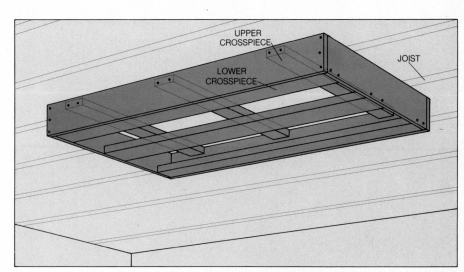

2 **Fastening the cabinets to the frame.** After fastening a row of cabinets together *(page 49, Step 1)*, attach hanging bars *(page 27)* inside the tops of each cabinet at front and back, corresponding with the positions of the lower crosspieces on the ceiling frame and then have helpers hold the cabinets up against the frame while you drill pilot holes. Locate these screw holes at the left and right ends of all the hanging strips and screw the cabinets to the crosspieces with 2-inch No. 8 screws. Fasten each back-to-back pair of cabinets together with two 1¼-inch No. 6 screws and cover the joints at the ceiling and the bottom of the hanging frame with moldings.

Cabinets that Blend an Appliance into a Room

A custom-built cabinet can make an appliance or fixture more attractive—and more useful. More attractive, because the cabinet either covers or camouflages a bulky machine and blends with the room's décor. More useful, because the cabinet provides storage above or below.

Kitchen appliances make especially good candidates for this treatment. In fact, some are designed specifically to fit into the standard array of kitchen cabinetry. A dishwasher matches the height and depth of a row of base cabinets and fits directly underneath a countertop; a cooktop must be fitted into a hole in a countertop.

Large appliances, such as refrigerators and wall ovens, must have specialized cabinets around them for a built-in effect. Any modern refrigerator that has bottom-mounted coils is easily enclosed in a cabinet *(page 58)* that frames the front of the appliance and provides a storage area above. A refrigerator that has back-mounted coils needs more clearance for ventilation—follow the manufacturer's recommendations for the cabinet dimensions. An oven cabinet *(page 58)* provides storage space above and below, and supports the oven as well.

Make the top for a refrigerator or oven cabinet level with the adjacent cabinet tops; if space between the adjacent cabinets and the ceiling is covered by a soffit or cornice molding, use the same covering over the appliance cabinet.

Because either a refrigerator or oven cabinet may be taller and wider than a standard doorway, plan to assemble them in the kitchen. If you design either of them to reach all the way to the ceiling, make the diagonal measurements of the cabinet sides 1 inch less than the height of the room *(page 59)*; whatever the depth of the sides, this limitation will permit you to tilt the cabinet to an upright position without hitting the ceiling.

A smaller, easier-to-build cabinet—for a fixture rather than an appliance—is the radiator cover shown on these pages. This cover is little more than a box that fits over the radiator and against the wall,

and has perforated aluminum sheeting tacked to a front frame.

Since any cover cuts a radiator's efficiency, choose a sheeting with a pattern of large holes or openings, to allow as much air flow as possible. In addition, tack solid-aluminum sheeting to the underside of the top and, if possible, to the wall behind the radiator—it will increase efficiency by reflecting heat. Both kinds of sheeting are available at hardware stores and building-supply dealers. Vary the design of a radiator cabinet to suit your taste and needs: You can, for example, cut an opening in the top for an inset of perforated aluminum sheeting, and hinge a small section of the top for easy access to the radiator valve.

The techniques for building cabinets for large appliances are those described earlier in this chapter, slightly modified to accommodate the shape and function of each appliance. Refrigerator and oven cabinets should be stained or painted in place; radiator covers can be finished before they are installed.

A Cover for a Radiator

1 **Making the face frame.** Glue and butt-nail two horizontal rails between two vertical stiles. Make the assembly from ¾-by-2 lumber, with the stiles cut 3 inches longer than the height of the radiator, and the rails 2 inches longer than the total width of the radiator and valve. Set the first rail between the tops of the stiles and the second at least 3 inches from the floor for proper air flow; if the bottom of the radiator is less than 3 inches above the floor, position the rail to leave the radiator partially exposed.

With the frame face down, nail perforated aluminum sheeting over the framed opening.

2 **Attaching the sides and brace.** Nail the stiles to the front edges of ¾-inch plywood sides, which are cut to the height of the stiles and 1½ inches wider than the depth of the radiator from the wall. Fasten a 1-by-4 brace across the interior of the cover, flush with the top and ½ inch in from the back, using four nails driven through the sides and into the ends of the brace.

Cut a ¾-inch plywood top 2 inches wider and 1 inch deeper than the unit. Finish the front and side edges *(page 12)* and tack plain aluminum sheeting to the underside of the top.

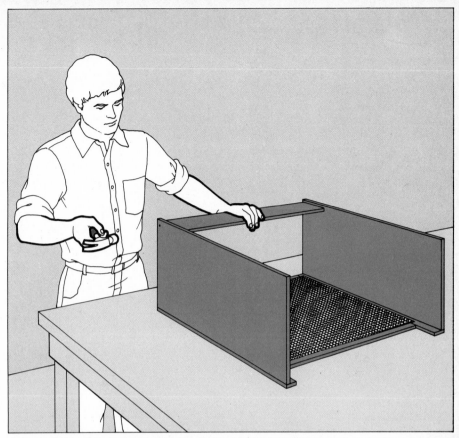

3 **Attaching the top.** Set the back of the top flush with the back edges of the sides, and fasten the top in place with nails driven at 8-inch intervals into the sides, front rail and back brace.

Cut 1-by-2 cleats to the height of the sides, and nail them to studs or attach them to wallboard with toggle bolts, locating them just inside the points where the sides of the cover will fit. After scribing and shaping the sides of the cover to fit the wall and baseboard *(page 48)*, screw the unit to each cleat.

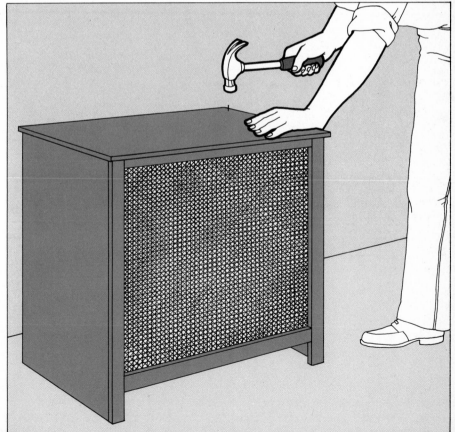

Building In
Large Kitchen Appliances

A built-in refrigerator. This enclosure is essentially a top cabinet (*page 16*). Cut each of the sides to the distance between the back of the refrigerator-door gasket and the wall, and to the height of the adjacent cabinet tops; if adjacent cabinets reach the ceiling, cut each side so that its diagonal measurement equals the height of the room less 1 inch (*page 59, Step 1*).

Cut a top and shelf to the width of the refrigerator plus 5 inches. In each side, cut a rabbet for the top and a dado that will set the shelf at the level above the top of the refrigerator recommended by the manufacturer. Then cut a back to fit the space between the shelf and the top, add a hanging bar (*page 27, Step 4*) and cut a rabbet in each side to hold the back. Glue and nail the pieces together (*pages 26-29*).

Use ¾-by-2 lumber for the stiles and rails of the face frame. Install doors (*pages 37-41*) on the section of the cabinet above the refrigerator. Then fasten 1½-by-¾ cleats to the inside bottoms of both sides, and drive nails through the cleats into the floor. Fasten the top of the cabinet to the wall by nailing through the hanging bar into studs.

A built-in wall oven. This floor-to-ceiling cabinet combines features of base and wall-mounted cabinets. The sides are 2 inches deeper than the oven, with diagonal measurements that match the height of the room less 1 inch (*page 59, Step 1*). The back is the same height, and as wide as the oven plus 5 inches, with a hanging bar fastened across the top and a hole for the oven's electrical plug cut at the location specified by the manufacturer.

Inside the cabinet a top, a bottom and an intermediate shelf fit into the sides: the bottom fits into dadoes 1¼ inches above the bottom edges, the shelf into dadoes ½ inch above the top of the oven, and the top into rabbets cut across the top edges. Rabbets along the back edges of the sides receive the back of the cabinet. The face frame is made of ¾-by-2 lumber except for the rail beneath the oven, which is ¾-by-4 lumber. The entire cabinet rests on a base 5¼ inches high.

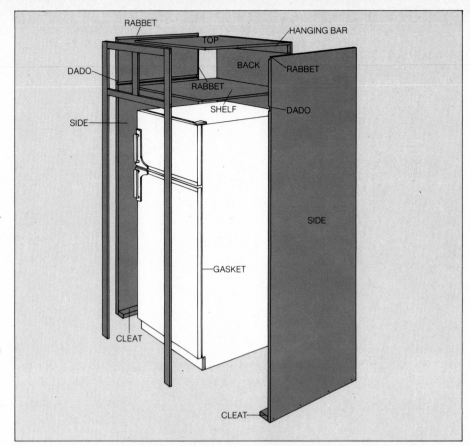

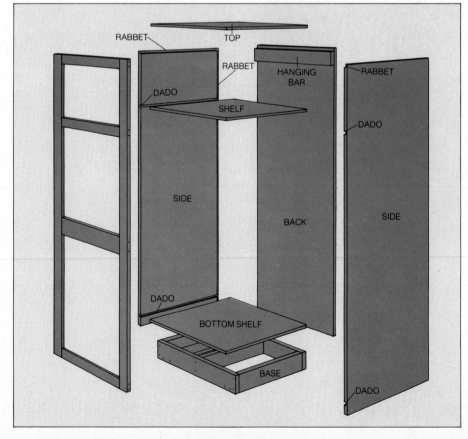

Making an Oven Cabinet

1 **Measuring and cutting the sides.** Mark the depth of a side on the top edge of a plywood panel and have a helper hold the end of a steel tape ruler to the mark. Extend the tape to the height of the room less 1 inch, swing the tape to the side of the panel and mark the point where the tape meets the side edge. From this mark, measure and mark the depth of the side, then connect all the marks and cut the side. Cut the second side, cut the remaining pieces as shown in the anatomy on page 58, bottom, and assemble the cabinet by the methods indicated on pages 26-29.

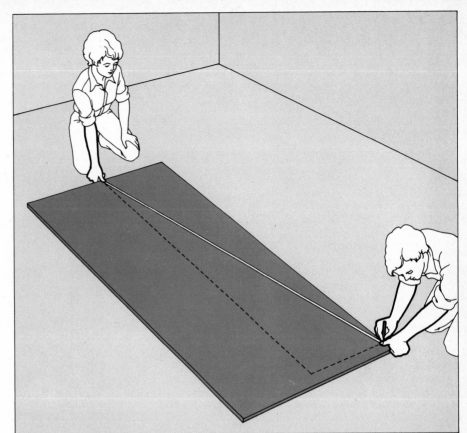

2 **Making the face frame.** Glue and butt-nail four rails between two stiles. Start this part of the job by cutting stiles of ¾-by-2 lumber to the height of the cabinet. Cut the rails to the width of the oven plus 5 inches. Make three rails of ¾-by-2 lumber, and nail the first between the tops of the stiles, the second between the bottoms, and the third ½ inch above the top of the oven opening. Cut the fourth rail of ¾-by-4 lumber, and fasten it at the bottom of the oven opening. Attach the face frame to the cabinet (*page 33, Step 8*).

Cut two 2-by-4 supports to the depth of the cabinet sides; the oven will rest on these supports.

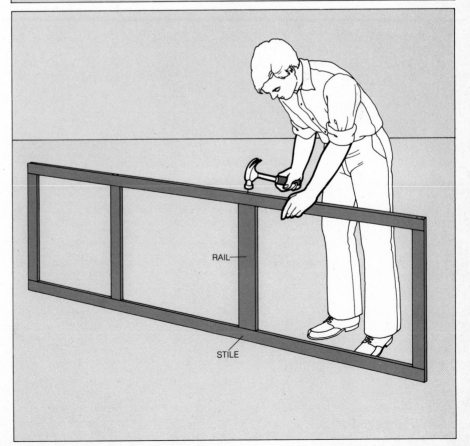

RAIL

STILE

3 **Nailing in the oven supports.** Hold a support flat inside the cabinet from front to back, with its upper corner against an upper corner of the rail at the bottom of the oven opening, and drive two nails through the rail and two through the cabinet back, into the ends of the support. Attach the second support on the other side of the cabinet. Then cut two 1-by-3 cleats to the inside width of the cabinet.

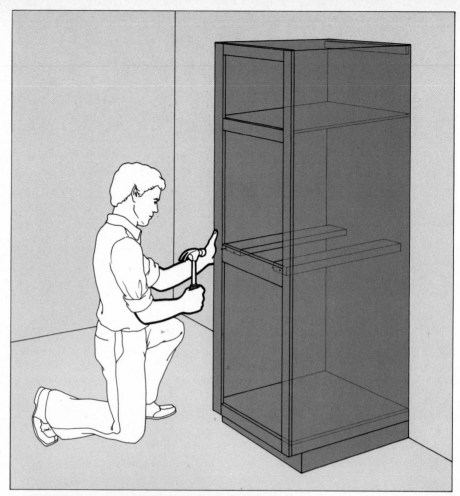

4 **Installing cleats for extra strength.** Hold a cleat inside the cabinet with its ends against the sides, its face against the bottoms of the supports and its edge against the front rail, and drive two nails through each side of the cabinet into the ends of the cleat. Attach the second cleat under the 2-by-4s at the back of the cabinet.

Install doors above the oven opening and either doors or drawers below (*pages 34-41*); fasten the cabinet to its base (*page 52, Steps 1-3*) and to the studs behind it (*page 47, Steps 2-3*).

Wall-to-Wall Storage

The ultimate in built-in cabinetry is the storage wall, created by building vertical partitions out from one wall in a room and filling the space between them with shelves, hanger-rods and drawers. The storage wall holds more than separate cabinets can hold and, fitted with doors and drawers, it becomes part of the room, ready for any covering from a coat of paint to a supergraphic *(page 71)*.

The plywood frame shown on these pages makes a simple but versatile skeleton for such a storage wall. The entire structure, made almost entirely of ¾-inch plywood, can be cut with a circular or table saw. Its partitions can be placed for convenience anywhere between side walls; normally the partitions are ceiling-high, but some are shorter to accommodate a long shelf above. Convenience also determines how far they protrude from the old wall, but a depth of 2 feet permits two partitions to be cut from a single 4-by-8 plywood panel.

Hanger-rods or shelves can span any interval between partitions but need intermediate support brackets at least every 32 inches. At the partitions, hanger-rods are best supported by special end brackets available in hardware stores. A series of shelves is supported by shelf standards screwed to the partitions; a single shelf is supported at a partition by toenailing or by an extra 1-by-2 cleat.

Anatomy of a useful wall. This room-width array of built-in shelves, drawers and hanger-rods is divided neatly into vertical compartments by partitions that are held to the floor and wall by cleats. Bottoms for the compartments extend over a toe kick, while a soffit borders the entire assembly at the ceiling. A short partition, convenient but just as easily omitted, helps support a long shelf and hanger-rod that are elsewhere braced by full-height partitions and support brackets fastened to the back wall *(inset)*.

This combination of partitions, shelves, drawers and hanger-rods, however, is only an example—the compartments can be of any width and number to accommodate anything from skis to barbells. Doors can be attached to partition stiles to cover all or some of the compartments.

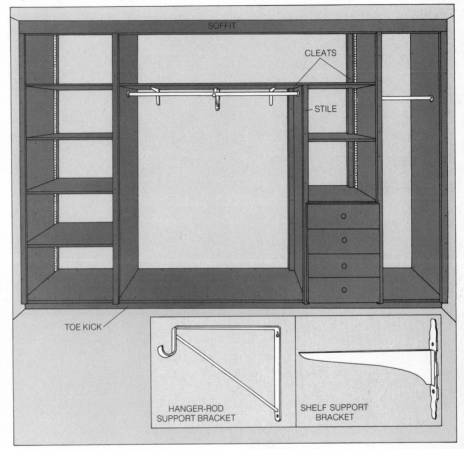

Erecting a Storage Wall

1 **Testing the walls for squareness.** After removing the baseboard around the storage area, set a steel square on the floor at the corner of the back wall and each side wall, with the 16-inch leg of the square flat against the back wall. If either end of the 24-inch leg is more than ¼ inch from the side wall, mark the entire deviation with a line on the floor. Following the same procedure, draw deviation lines at the corners of the ceiling. If the corners are square, measure the length of the back wall; if they are not, measure the shortest distance between the ends of the deviation lines.

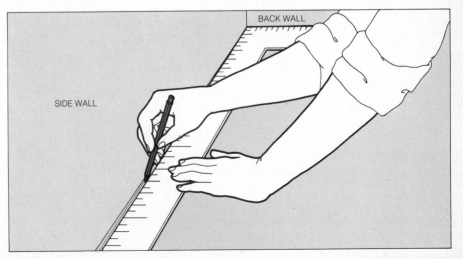

2 Dividing and marking the space. Divide the distance measured in Step 1 into vertical sections, mark the sections off at the top and bottom of the back wall and snap chalk lines between the marks. Use the 24-inch leg of a steel square to extend each vertical line along the floor.

3 Installing partition cleats. For all but the two side-wall partitions nail 1-by-2 cleats to the floor and wall. Make wall cleats the height of the partitions, floor cleats 3¾ inches shorter than the partition depth. Locate the cleats ⅜ inch from the partition lines. If a wall cleat does not fall over a stud, fasten it to the wall with toggle bolts (*page 50, Step 2*) at 1-foot intervals.

4 Installing the partitions. With a helper, nail each interior partition to the wall cleats and floor cleats at 6-inch intervals; at wall cleats that are fastened with toggle bolts, use 1½-inch No. 8 screws rather than nails. Make the partitions, including two for the side walls, of ¾-inch plywood cut 1 inch shorter than the height of the room, and with a notch 3¾ inches deep and 4 inches long at the bottom front corner.

If the corners of the room are square, set each side-wall partition directly against the wall and nail through it into the studs. If the corners are not square, tack shingle shims to the partition at the top and bottom and at 2-foot intervals to compensate for the deviation, and nail the partitions in place through the shims and into the studs.

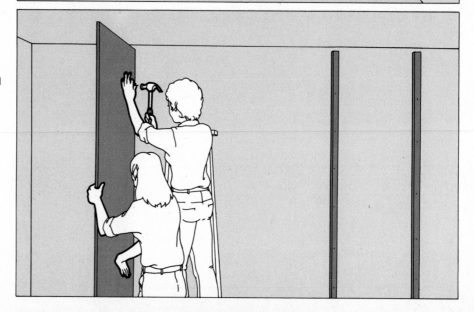

5 **Installing the bottom cleats.** Nail 1-by-2 cleats, cut to fit the sides and back of each section, to the partitions and to the studs of the back wall, with the tops of the cleats flush with the tops of the partition notches.

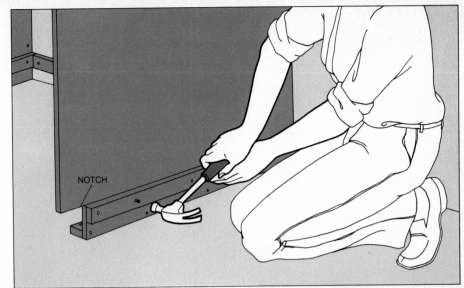

6 **Making a toe kick.** Nail a board, 4 inches wide and cut to fit between the side walls, into the notches at the bottoms of the partitions. If you must use two pieces to span the distance, butt their inner ends at the edge of a partition; nail the end of one piece to the partition and the end of the other to a cleat (*inset*).

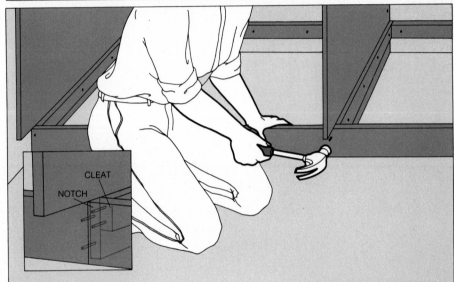

7 **Flooring the vertical sections.** Nail plywood bottom boards to the cleats at 8-inch intervals. Cut these boards to the full width and depth of each section and cut a notch in each board to fit it around a vertical wall cleat.

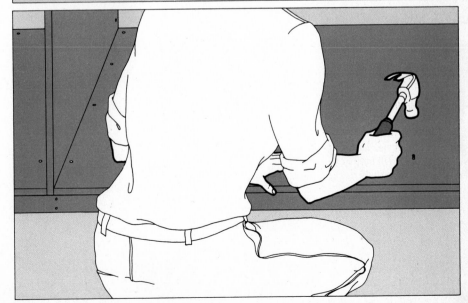

8 **Installing the soffit.** Nail a board, 4 inches wide and cut to fit between the side walls, to the top edges of the partitions. If you must use two pieces to span the distance, butt the ends at a partition edge and fasten a 1-by-2 block to one side of the partition as an additional nailing surface for the end of one soffit piece.

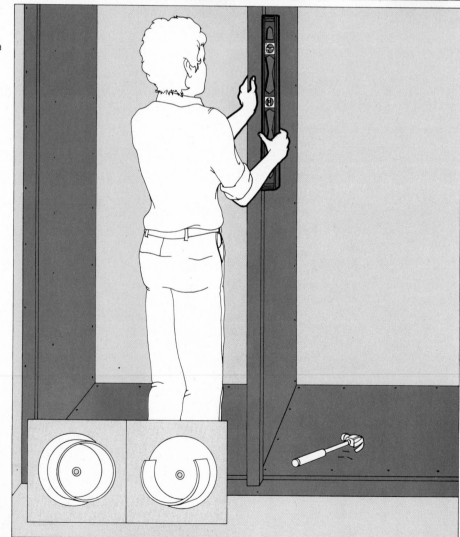

9 **Framing the partitions.** Using a single nail, tack a stile over the exposed front edge of each partition; check the stile for plumb, then nail it permanently in place at 10-inch intervals. On interior partitions, center the stiles over the partition edges; on side-wall partitions set the edge of a stile against the side wall.

Install shelves, drawers and doors by the methods shown in this chapter. Use end brackets (*inset*) to install hanger-rods at partitions.

Making the House a "Complete Work of Art"

The fact that built-ins save space is their obvious advantage. By framing in odd nooks and crannies, they provide shelves, drawers, tables, seating and even beds at no loss of existing open space. But such utility only partly explains why they have become prized features in today's homes. After all, these functions have been served for millennia by movable furniture. Even built-in kitchen cabinets were unusual until the 1900s—supplies were kept in freestanding cupboards, and the work surface was the kitchen table. (The Sears, Roebuck catalogue was still listing such cupboards in the 1970s.)

Built-ins have taken over, with the acceptance of a 20th Century concept of the dwelling place: the "organic" design preached by the great American architect Frank Lloyd Wright. Although he built only a few dozen very expensive houses, Wright's ideas have come to influence modern homes of every size and style—brick colonial as well as chrome-and-glass modern.

Wright believed that land, house and furnishings had to be a single unit, the outdoors flowing inside through broad expanses of window, the interior a unified series of spaces unbroken by enclosures but subtly divided by partial walls—and built-ins. "The very chairs and tables, cabinets and musical instruments, where practicable, are of the building itself," he wrote in 1910, adding, "this will become a tradition." And so it has, helping make the home handsome, practical and comfortable—the "complete work of art" that Wright envisioned.

Quick-change art. Even the paintings are built in—sliding into and out of view on ceiling tracks—in a room that has built-in seating, table and cabinet.

Dwellings Unified with Their Furnishings

Most people use built-in furniture to take advantage of—or compensate for—unusual features of the house structure. Thus, awkward windows and angles can become comfortable seating areas, as in the examples opposite.

But built-ins are more than quick solutions to architectural problems. A bed that seems to float just off the floor *(below)* emphasizes the spaciousness of a conventional room. And furniture integrated so completely into the structure of the house that it becomes a recess in a wall *(right)* gives those who use it a welcome sense of intimacy and security.

Wooden nook. A cozy breakfast area carved out of a wall is set off from the rest of the kitchen by the maple butcher block that forms its table, benches, walls and surrounding trim. Built in with it is a family data center *(right)*; the space within the walls is used for storage.

Space platform. The bedroom of a remodeled brownstone joins bed and storage compartments in a low platform. Hardware in the bed well raises the mattress for easy linen changing. Side soffit lighting makes the unit seem to float.

Seating shelf. Designed as an extension of the original whitewashed plaster walls and hearth, the new cushion seating in this Sardinian villa is based on a broad shelf of rough plastered brick. Additional courses of brick create the tables.

Elevated sofa. Windows are brought to eye level by the ingenious device of raising a curved bench on a platform covered with carpeting. The curved shape of the seating, repeating that of the arched windows, groups guests within comfortable conversation range. And the ends of the curve cover vents of the heating system.

New Dimensions
with Room Dividers

The old way to subdivide the space in a home was with walls and doors. The resulting rooms were clearly defined and private but often depressingly confined if small, unsociably cold if large. The new way uses built-ins as dividers. They partition space into manageable, intimate units without cutting it up, leaving a sense of freedom and interweaving to create a unified pattern for living. And they do double duty, serving as screening, storage, seating or service areas.

Wall from a factory. A spectacular assemblage of stripes, clouds and a mirror-like surface surrounds a room divider between sleeping and dressing areas. It is a grid of industrial shelving that is partially sheathed in perforated metal.

Room within a room. Japanese-style sliding doors, covered in discreetly patterned cotton, subdivide a large living room into two social areas. The doors and track housing are maple, to match the window frames and sofa bases.

Multiple division. A series of dividers and platforms shapes a large, open interior. The triangular divider at left, wrapped in plastic laminate, is echoed by a storage cabinet in the foreground and a planter at center. The cylinders, of red-lacquered masonry, enclose a supporting column (*foreground*) and a chimney flue for the fireplace. Black marble covers platforms that create one seating area and surround another.

Storage Custom-made for the Things Stored

Storage cabinets are traditional built-ins, but the examples pictured on these pages are special. Each unit has been custom-designed with specific possessions in mind—for example, slotted racks for records *(right)*, spaces cut to the shape of kitchen equipment *(below, right)*, many drawers in graduated depths for different categories of clothing *(opposite)*—all in the hope of inducing users to put away things that are not in use.

In addition, each of these solutions makes economical use of space: where cabinets are tucked against existing walls, the storage function is unobtrusive, because the furniture becomes part of the room's basic architecture.

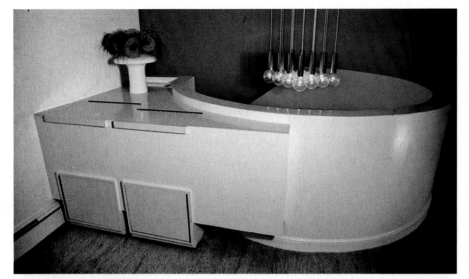

Stairway stowage. In this living room, the odd corner created by a curving staircase becomes a built-in stereo center. The cabinet, of birch veneer painted the same dull finish as the plaster walls, has a hatch on top and doors in front.

Shaped scullery. Plastic, scooped out to the individual shapes of the household pots and pans, provides both easy storage and a whimsical mural. The designer, using an electric cutting tool, gave each of the 3-by-10-foot blocks a convex or concave face, then carved niches. The blocks are stacked against the wall and ceiling with a fit snug enough to hold them in place.

2

Furniture to Fit the House

A miniature sawmill for precision cuts. A table saw fitted with a dado head *(page 24)* makes quick and accurate work of cutting stepped rabbet and grooved dado joints. The width of a cut depends upon the number of narrow inner blades, called chippers, that are sandwiched between two circular outer blades, called cutters; paper washers between chippers create fine width adjustments. When the entire assembly has been mounted, a wide-slotted plate *(to right of blade)* screws onto the table around it.

There are several reasons for building-in furniture, some esthetic and some dollars-and-cents practical. To an architect, the value of built-in benches, sofas, tables and even beds lies in the ease with which they can be integrated into the plan of the house, so that furnishings become one with the fundamental structures of walls, floors and ceilings, and the entire design is unified.

A plywood strip placed wall to wall across an alcove creates a bench that is more likely to appear to belong in the space than would separate, movable chairs or settee. It seems to fit because it does fit; you can construct a 14-foot bench almost as readily as one 4 feet long, suiting the scale of furniture to the scale of the room (and to the scale of the occupants, for you can adjust the dimensions of seats and tables to the dimensions of their users).

Built-in furniture looks like part of the house not only because it fits but because it is part of the house—a practical advantage on many counts. To a large extent a built-in is held together by the house structure, getting its strength and rigidity from the studs and joists of wall and floor. As a result, it is exceptionally sturdy; a built-in bunk bed withstands juvenile jouncing better than most store-bought bunks, and small children can clamber over screwed-down benches and table without being spilled onto the floor.

The strength contributed by the house framing eliminates the need for the precise joinery of freestanding furniture. The techniques involved are those of the carpenter rather than the cabinetmaker. Thick, sturdy lumber is used, and most pieces are nailed or screwed together (and to the house). Elaborate systems of springs are unnecessary; foam cushions or mattresses make plain wooden bench structures into comfortable sofas or beds. Similarly unnecessary—and generally undesirable—is ordinary upholstery; standard cushions are readily fitted with homemade or store-bought covers, and built-in sofas often are totally integrated into house design with coverings of carpeting run up from the floor and over them.

Because built-in furniture is simpler than freestanding pieces in so many ways, it is easy to build. It is also economical. A homemade sofa—of plywood, 2-by-4s and 1-by-2s screwed to the wall and covered with foam cushions and carpeting *(pages 84-89)*—may cost only a fifth or even a tenth as much as a standard living-room piece.

This economy and simplicity make built-in furniture frequent choices for the less formal areas of a home: benches and tables for family dining, benches in halls, sofas in recreation rooms and vacation cabins, beds in children's rooms. But appropriately designed, built-ins adorn any room, and many of today's stylish homes *(pages 65-71)* are furnished with little else.

Simple yet Versatile Seating: The Bench

A built-in bench, bed or sofa is easier to build than its freestanding counterpart, and a built-in bench is the easiest of all. It is also the most versatile. A shelflike bench provides seating in an out-of-the-way alcove. A boxlike storage bench holds toys or linens without encroaching on precious floor space. More elaborate benches, with backrests and arms, can turn a kitchen corner into a breakfast nook complete with built-in table (pages 96-101), or create a handy spot in a porch or entryway to pull off muddy galoshes.

All of these benches can be assembled with simple dado and rabbet joints, cut with a router or a table saw and strengthened by concealed glue blocks and hardware reinforcements. The easiest assembly is little more than a shelf fitted between the walls of an alcove—a plywood seat supported by three 2-by-4s, called ledgers, that are fastened to the

back and sides of the alcove, and to a fourth 2-by-4 across the front.

This frame provides all the necessary support for a bench less than 42 inches wide. A wider bench must have interior framing (Step 4, opposite) below the seat and one or more legs: a single leg at the center of the front support for a bench 42 to 84 inches wide; two legs, spaced 42 inches apart, for a bench wider than 84 inches. Any of these benches—and any other bench you build—can be used for storage if you sheathe the front with plywood and hinge the seat (page 79).

A bench fastened to a single wall rather than set into an alcove calls for more elaborate framing. The storage bench on pages 76-79, for example, rests upon a ledger, a framework of 2-by-4s, and a set of three 2-by-4 plates anchored to the floor; the interior frame is covered on all its exposed sides by a plywood skin.

A special problem in assembling a built-in bench is leveling the seat. In a bench built on site, you solve the problem by adjusting the framing pieces as you go along. For an alcove bench, simply level the ledgers (Step 1, below). Leveling a bench that is attached to one wall and partially supported by vertical framing is trickier. The heights of the vertical pieces must be set individually, either by using a level to determine their heights before cutting them (page 76, Step 2) or by scribing the cut supports (page 83).

All built-in benches are anchored to the studs of a wall with lag bolts or ¼-inch wood screws. Find the studs by the techniques described on page 46, and mark their locations on the walls. Most benches are between 17 and 22 inches in height; if you plan to use the bench with a standard 29-inch table, make the seat 18 inches high.

Building an Alcove Bench

1 Installing the ledgers. Cut a 2-by-4 to fit between the side walls of the alcove and groove it with dadoes 1½ inches wide, ⅜ inch deep and 36 inches apart for interior crosspieces. Level the back ledger on the back wall ¾ inch below seat height, and fasten the ledger to the studs of the wall with ¼-inch lag bolts.

For the side ledgers, cut two 2-by-4s to the seat depth less 2⅝ inches. Butt these ledgers against the back ledger along the side walls, level them, and attach them to the wall studs with lag bolts. Toenail them to the back ledger.

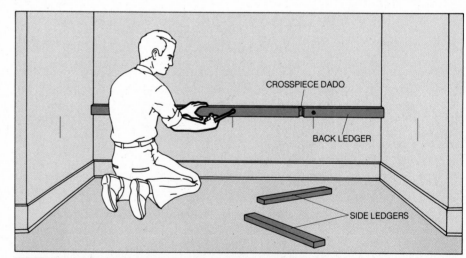

CROSSPIECE DADO

BACK LEDGER

SIDE LEDGERS

2 The front support. Glue and screw across the side ledgers a 2-by-4 that is cut as long as the back ledger, is dadoed like it for crosspieces and has end rabbets 1½ inches wide and ⅜ inch deep. If legs are needed, make dadoes for them in the front support; such leg dadoes should be 3½ inches wide, ⅜ inch deep and no more than 42 inches apart. In this example, the front support is dadoed for one leg at the center.

3 Attaching legs. If legs are needed, make each one from a 2-by-4, cut to fit between the top of the front support and the floor, and rabbeted at one end 3½ inches wide and ¾ inch deep. Fit the rabbet into the leg dado in the front support and secure the rabbeted end with glue and screws. Toenail the bottom end to the floor.

4 Adding crosspieces. Cut 2-by-4s to fit between the dadoes in the back ledger and the dadoes in the front support. Glue the crosspieces into the dadoes, then toenail them to the back ledger and face-nail them to the front support.

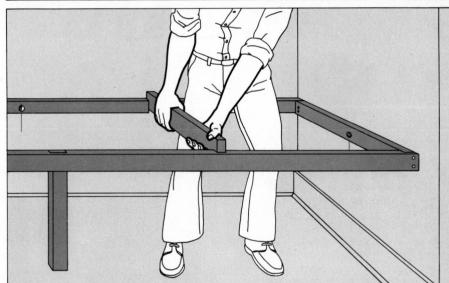

5 Installing the seat. Using the techniques on page 53, scribe and cut a plywood seat to fit the contours of the alcove and overhang the front support by 2 inches; glue the seat to the frame and fasten it with finishing nails. Conceal the joint between the seat and the walls with strips of quarter-round molding (*page 47*). For an uncushioned seat, attach a ¾-inch nosing (*page 12, Step 6*) to the front of the seat; if you plan to use cushions, use a 1¾-inch nosing, which will create a lip above the edge of the seat.

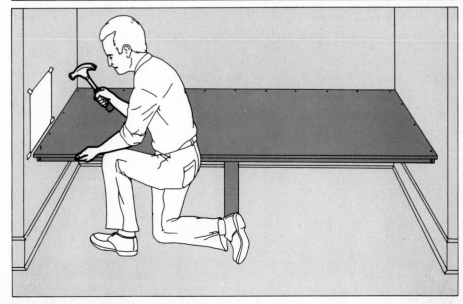

A Storage Bench
with Interior Framing

1 Setting the plates. Cut two 2-by-4s, each 4¼ inches shorter than the seat depth. Cut a 2-by-4 that is 1½ inches shorter than the bench length. Nail the plates to the floor, one end of each short plate perpendicular to the wall and the other butting against an end of the long plate.

For the back ledger and the front support, cut two 2-by-4s three inches shorter than the front plate. Cut 1½-inch dadoes 12 inches from each end of these pieces, and fasten the back ledger to the wall *(page 74, Step 1)*.

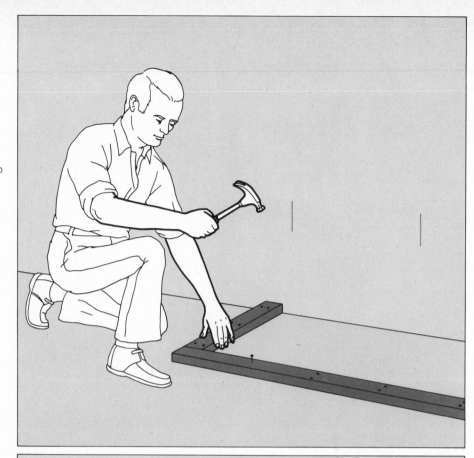

2 Measuring for the vertical supports. Set one end of a level on top of each end of the ledger and measure the height of the level from the floor directly in front of the plate frame. Subtract 5¾ inches from each of the measurements and cut two sections of 2-by-4 to these lengths. Glue and toenail these 2-by-4 supports on top of the plate at the two front corners.

3 **Framing around corner cleats.** Using a cardboard shield to protect the wall, nail 2-by-4 side
supports, ¾ inch shorter than the bench
depth, to the ends of the back ledger, and glue
them to the tops of the front vertical supports.
Set 6-inch 2-by-2 cleats overlapping the joints between the side and vertical supports, use glue
and nails to fasten them in place, then glue and
nail the front support to the front edges of the
corner cleats *(inset)*.

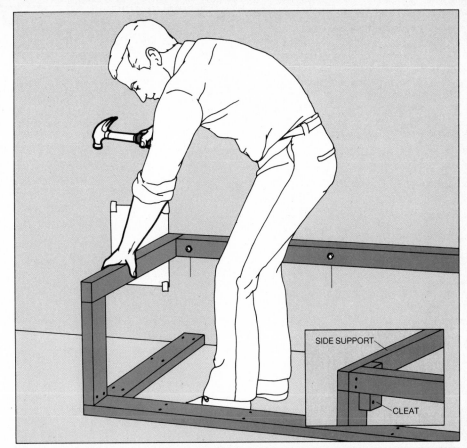

SIDE SUPPORT

CLEAT

4 **Installing the lid supports.** Cut two 2-by-4s to fit
into the dadoes of the ledger and the front
support, and cut a 1½-inch dado 3¾ inches from
an end of each piece; glue and nail the pieces
into place so that their dadoes are at the back of
the bench and facing each other. Glue and
nail a third 2-by-4 into the dadoes of the lid support. Reinforce the joints of all three pieces
with cleats *(Step 3, above)* or with metal corner
braces, available at hardware stores.

Cover the sides and front of the bench with pieces
of ¾-inch plywood, scribing the back edges
to the wall *(page 48)*.

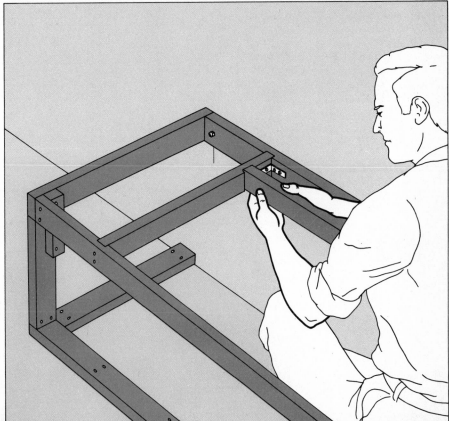

5 **Marking the seat.** Cut a seat of ¾-inch plywood to fit flush with the sides of the bench and to overhang the front by 1 inch; scribe and plane the back of the seat so that it fits flush against the wall (*page 48*). At several points, measure the distances from the sides of the bench to the center of the interior side supports and from the back of the bench to 1 inch beyond the interior back support; transfer the points to the plywood seat and, using a utility knife and a straight-edge, connect them with lines for the back and sides of the lid.

6 **Cutting the sides of the lid.** Clamp the seat to a workbench with the line marking one side of the lid overhanging the edge of the bench and, using a straightedge guide and a circular saw, cut along the line from the front of the seat to a point 1 inch short of the corner of the lid, to allow space for a precise corner cutout. Complete the cut with a keyhole saw and repeat the procedure on the opposite side of the seat.

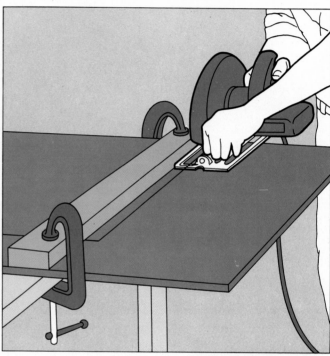

7 **Cutting the back of the lid.** Reposition the seat on the workbench so that the line marking the back edge of the lid overhangs the edge of the bench. Attach a guide beside the mark and set the saw with its base against the guide and its blade about 3 inches in from one end of the line. Push the blade guard forward to expose the blade and tilt the saw onto the front edge of its base, lifting the blade clear of the wood. Turn the saw on and slowly lower the blade into the wood until the base rests flat. Hold the saw firmly—it will tend to bounce as it bites into the wood—and cut to a point 1 inch from the corner of the lid. Complete the cut at both ends of the line with a keyhole saw; the cutout will form the lid of the seat.

Use the saw to trim a strip from the back of the lid equal to 1½ inches plus the width of the piano hinge you will use to hinge the lid. Sand the inside edges of the seat and the edges of the lid.

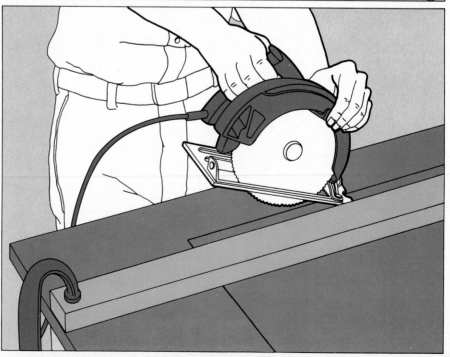

8 **Attaching the seat.** Attach the back of the seat to the top of the bench with glue and finishing nails. Cut two strips of ¾-inch lumber, each ¾ inch wide, to the length of the hinge line; using glue and sixpenny finishing nails, attach the strips to the hinge edges of the seat and the lid. The strips (inset) will provide a fastening surface for the screws of the hinge, which would not hold fast in the edges of the plywood.

9 **Hinging the lid.** Select a piano hinge that has ¾-inch leaves and, using a hacksaw, cut it to the length of the lid; fasten one leaf of the hinge to the wooden strip at the back of the lid. Set the lid upright at the back of its opening, center it with $\frac{1}{16}$-inch spacers wedged between its back corners and the seat, and have a helper hold it completely open so that you can fasten the other leaf of the hinge to the strip on the seat.

To finish the bench, countersink and putty all exposed nailheads, and attach ¾-inch nosings to the exposed edges of the seat and lid.

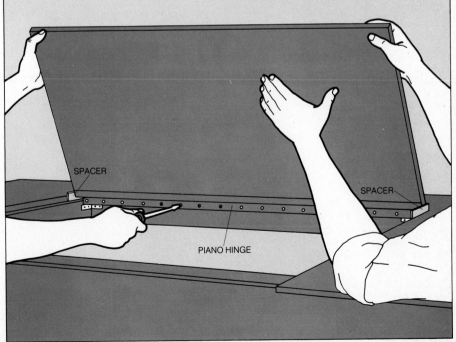

SPACER

SPACER

PIANO HINGE

A Bench with a Back and Arms

A bench built for heavy use—a porch seat, for example, or a bench in a dining area—is more elaborate than one used for occasional seating. Its frame is similar to those on the preceding pages, but the installation of the frame is trickier, and arms and a back rest make the completed bench more comfortable and inviting.

The example below is built as a freestanding unit, trimmed to fit the contours of its location, then anchored to the wall and floor. Using the same construction techniques, you can enhance the appearance of the bench by cutting its sides and back in curved or scrollwork shapes, using a high nosing to make a lip for seat cushions *(page 75)* or installing a sloped back *(page 86)*. For greater safety, round any sharp corners with a sander or a rasp.

Like any other built-in, a kitchen bench must be fitted to its room, but some proportions are standard. The most comfort-able depth for a seat with a back rest is between 16 and 22 inches; the height of the seat should be 10 to 12 inches lower than the table it faces. Armrests should rise between 8 and 10 inches above the seat; higher arms make access difficult between the bench and a table. And a standard back rest is 13 to 18 inches high, although you may prefer a higher one to create a secluded dining area.

For the bench built with its back against the wall, follow the construction techniques on these pages, with a few simple variations. First attach the back rest and a back ledger to the wall; then, working out from the wall, add sidepieces fitted to the contours of the floor. The lag bolts that fasten the back rest to the studs should be countersunk and concealed with prefabricated plugs called bungs or with homemade plugs cut from doweling or scrap lumber.

Anatomy of the bench. The 2-by-4 framework of this bench consists of a front support and a back ledger, dadoed at the center for an interior support and screwed to two side ledgers. Two plywood sides, shaped to form arms, rise from the floor; they are nailed to the side ledgers and screwed to the ends of the back ledger. Armrest caps are shaped from short lumber sections dadoed to fit the freestanding plywood side and rabbeted to fit the side against the wall. A plywood back rises from the bottom of the back ledger and fits into rabbets cut in the two sides.

A plywood seat, cantilevered 4 inches beyond the front support, rests on the frame and is glued to dadoes in the back and sides. One side of the bench is lag-bolted to a wall; the other is fastened to a 2-by-2 cleat nailed to the floor.

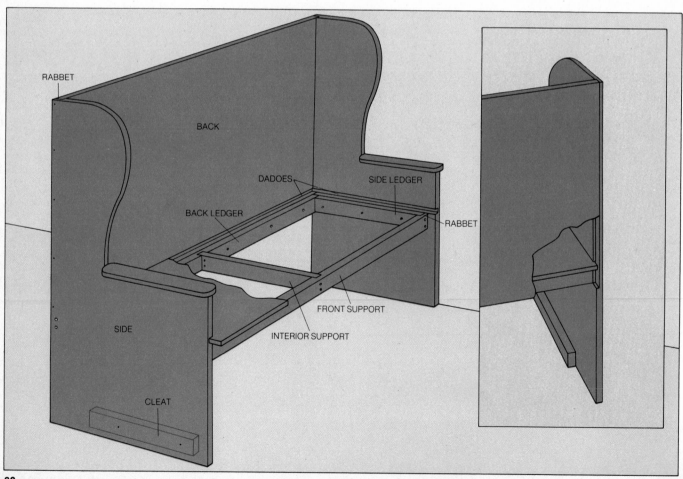

RABBET

BACK

DADOES

SIDE LEDGER

BACK LEDGER

RABBET

FRONT SUPPORT

SIDE

INTERIOR SUPPORT

CLEAT

Building the Bench

1 **Marking the pieces.** Cut two sidepieces of ¾-inch plywood, shape the top and front edges with a saber saw and, at the height of the seat, use a metal square and a utility knife to mark the outlines of a ¾-inch dado on each piece. Directly below each dado, mark the position of a 2-by-4 side ledger, 2¼ inches in from the back edge and 3⅝ inches in from the front. Finally, mark a line for a ¾-inch rabbet along the back of each piece, extending from the top corner to a point 3½ inches below the bottom of the dado.

Cut a plywood back with a height matching the sidepiece rabbets and a length ¾ inch shorter than the bench. Mark the back for a ¾-inch dado 3½ inches from the bottom, and mark the back-ledger position ⅜ inch in from each end.

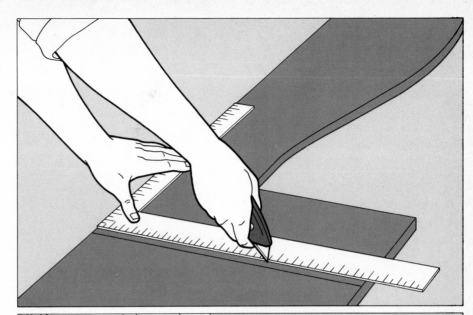

2 **Cutting joints for the back.** Use a router to cut rabbets to a depth of ⅜ inch on the side-pieces, then square the rounded ends of the rab-bets with a chisel. Set the bevel of the chisel blade facing the rabbet and tap the handle gently with a mallet to make a shallow cut, then set the bevel upward and drive the blade horizontally to shave out the bottom of the notch.

3 **Making supports for the seat.** Fasten ledgers to each sidepiece (*below, right*) and the back (*below*) by the following method: Cut ⅜-inch-deep dadoes in the sidepieces and back between the lines marked in Step 1 and cut 2-by-4s to the ledger lengths marked on the sides and back; notch the center of the back ledger with a dado 1½ inches wide and ⅜ inch deep. Secure the ledgers with glue and sixpenny nails.

Using a ³/₃₂-inch bit, drill two pilot holes through each sidepiece between the back of the side ledger and the rabbet.

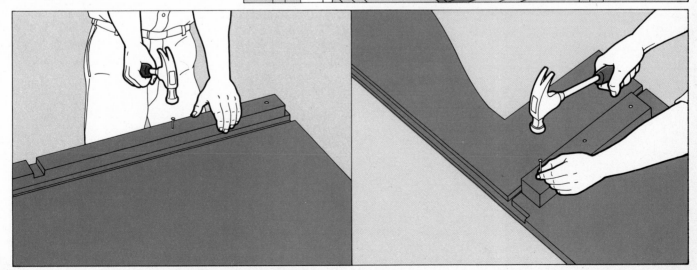

4 **Putting the pieces together.** Apply glue to the sidepiece rabbets and to the vertical edges of the back; then, working with a helper, fit the three pieces together, using corner clamps to hold them square. Tack the sides to the back along the rabbets with finishing nails at 6-inch intervals. Countersink two 2½-inch wood screws through the pilot holes in each side and into the ends of the back ledger.

Using the techniques shown on pages 74-75, Steps 2 and 4, complete the frame with a 2-by-4 front support and an interior support.

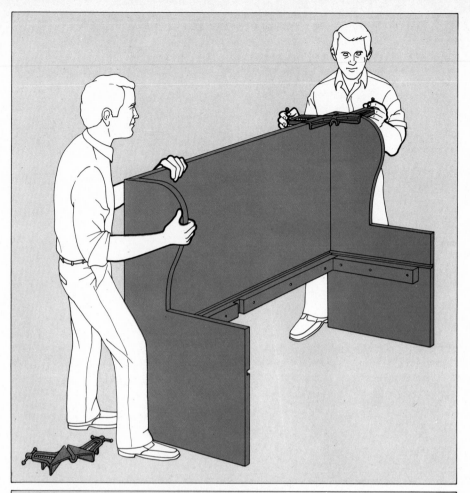

5 **Attaching the seat.** Cut a ¾-inch plywood seat to the length of the back dado and to the width of the side dadoes plus 2 inches; apply glue to the dadoes and the back and side edges of the seat, then slide the seat into place. At 8-inch intervals countersink finishing nails through the seat into the 2-by-4 framing beneath it. Glue and nail a 1-inch nosing to the front of the seat.

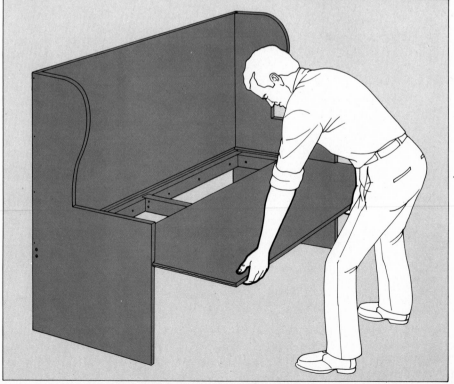

6 **Leveling the bench.** Set the end of the bench against the wall and, using a carpenter's level, shim the bench temporarily to level from side to side and from back to front. Scribe the bottoms of the sidepieces to conform to the floor, then tip the bench over and use a block plane to trim the plywood edges to the scribe marks. Reposition the bench and check it for level.

Mark the position for a 2-by-2 cleat set well within the edges of the outer sidepiece (page 80). Remove the bench and fasten the cleat to the floor with eightpenny nails.

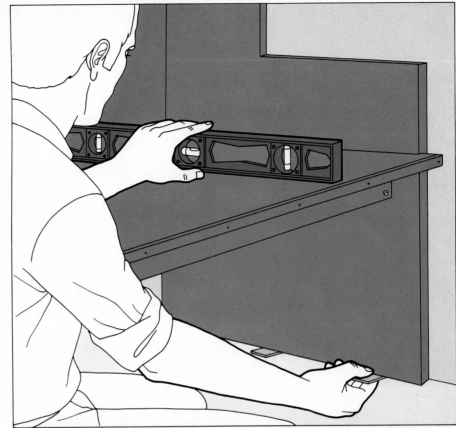

7 **Securing the bench.** Mark on the floor the location of the stud or studs behind the side of the bench, set the bench in place and use a combination square to extend the mark or marks vertically inside the bench and below the seat. Then mark points for lag bolts to secure the bench —two points 6 inches apart for a single stud, or one point 10 inches above the floor in each of two studs. Drill pilot holes and drive ¼-inch lag bolts through the sidepiece and into the studs; nail the other sidepiece to the floor cleat with sixpenny finishing nails at 6-inch intervals.

Make one armrest from a 1-by-3. Round its corners with a rasp or saber saw and, on its bottom, cut a dado stopped and squared ¾ inch short of one end (Step 2). Shape the other armrest from a 1-by-2 with one flat edge to fit against the wall and a stopped rabbet to fit the side of the bench. Attach the armrests to the sidepieces with glue and finishing nails.

Sofas Made to Order and Assembled on the Spot

More than its utilitarian cousin the bench, a built-in sofa meets the needs of interior design for odd spaces. A living room may have a nook too small or a wall too long for any store-bought sofa; a recreation room may have a corner for an inexpensive sofa that fills the space precisely. In many homes the answer to such problems is a custom-made sofa frame, blended into the room and fitted with cushions on the seat and back.

The construction described on these pages can be adapted to a variety of sofas. The furniture may be built between walls or flanked by end tables. The seat can be tilted 10° for comfort; two tilted seats can meet at a corner table. If the seat is made level, two can join at a corner without an end table; three level-seated sofas can form a U-shaped unit. For a sofa back, the house walls can support wedge-shaped cushions, 4 inches

thick at the top and 8 at the bottom, but most builders prefer a tilted back and straight cushions *(page 87)*.

In all these variations, the other sofa parts are fastened to the seat, which is supported in turn by the wall and floor *(below)*. Remove the baseboard *(page 8)* and fit the sides of an end table against the wall or scribe the sides of the table to fit around the baseboard *(page 48)*. For a sofa built at right angles to a wall, support the seat with ¾ inch boards fastened to the floor with 1-by-2 cleats, and cover the back of the sofa and end tables with plywood. The edges of these tables and of the sofa seat will be marked by long lines of rough plywood, which must be covered before the sofa is finished. Use veneer tape for a sofa that will have a natural finish, edge bands for one that will be painted *(page 12)*.

It is easy, but not essential, to use the

standard dimensions of factory-made sofas—generally a height and depth of 30 inches and a length of 75. If you want a sofa with unusual dimensions, upholsterers will make cushions to your order almost as cheaply as the standard sizes, and give you a broader selection of fabrics and foam grades.

Polyurethane foam is the material most often used for cushions. It is rated by density and compressibility. Buy foam with a density of at least 1.5 pounds per cubic foot—the denser foam is, the longer it lasts—and do not use foam that has sand mixed into it to increase its density. Foam compressibility, which can vary greatly between pieces of the same density, determines how comfortable the foam will be. Most people prefer a compressibility of 35 pounds—the weight required to squeeze a 2-foot square to three fourths its thickness.

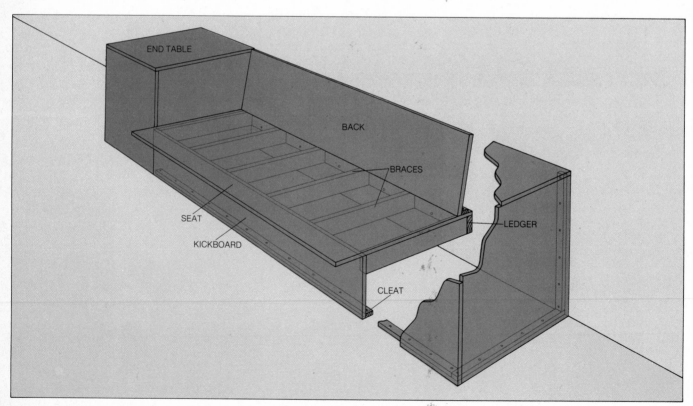

Anatomy of a built-in sofa. The sizes of the seat, back and end tables of this sofa can be modified to fit almost any space. A 1-by-12 kickboard fastened to the floor, a set of 2-by-4 braces and a ledger attached to the wall support the seat, which in turn provides the base for an angled back. The end tables, which may be any height, conceal the ends of the frame; in other arrangements, end tables join sofa sections at a corner or along a wall.

Building a Seat

1 **Making the frame.** Cut a 1-by-12 kickboard and a 2-by-4 ledger to the length of the seat; cut 2-by-4 braces 2¼ inches shorter than the depth of the seat. For a level seat, cut both ends of each brace square; for an angled seat, cut the ends parallel to one another but at an angle of about 2½° to the face, following a cutting line (*inset*) marked with a T bevel. Butt-nail the braces to the back of the kickboard at intervals of approximately 16 inches. Butt-nail the ledger to the other ends of the braces.

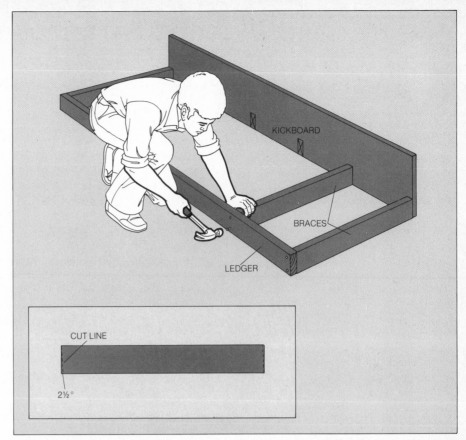

2 **Nailing the floor cleat.** Using a carpenter's square, straightedge and tape measure, mark a line on the floor at the location of the rear edge of the kickboard. Cut a 1-by-2 to the width of the sofa and nail it to the floor directly behind the line at 6-inch intervals.

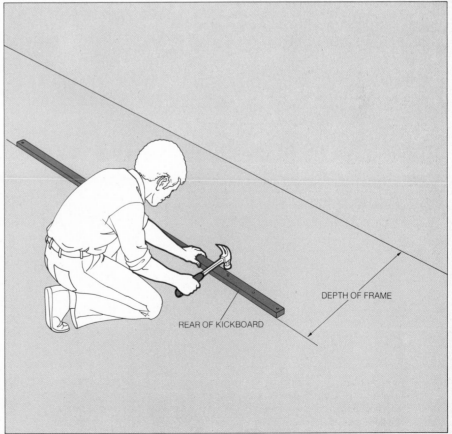

3 Fastening the frame in place. Draw a line on the wall at the kickboard height for a level seat, or 1½ inches lower for an angled seat. With a helper, set the ledger in place with its top directly under the line and nail it to each wall stud, then nail the bottom of the kickboard to the floor cleat at 6-inch intervals.

For the seat, cut a rectangle of plywood as long as the frame and 6 inches deeper; use finishing nails to nail it to the ledger and to the braces at 18-inch intervals.

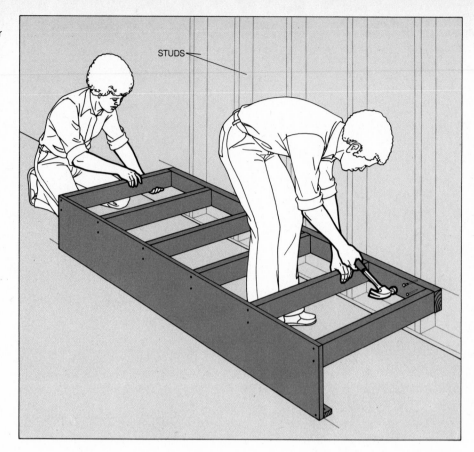

Setting In a Back

1 Positioning the back. Cut a plywood back to the length of the seat and about 16 inches high, set it in place at the back of the seat and slide its bottom forward until its angle matches that of a T bevel set at 100°. Check the angle along the entire back, then use a pencil to trace the bottom edge of the back on the seat.

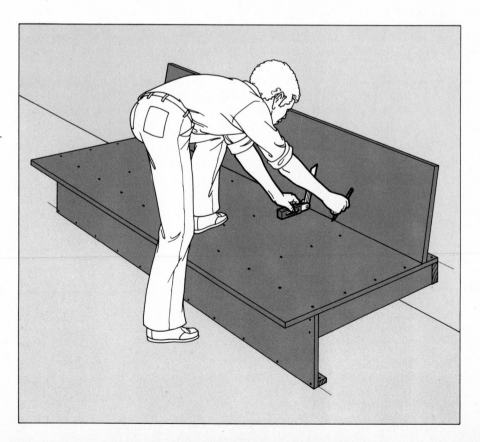

2 **Securing the back.** Slide a 1-by-2 cleat behind
and against the back, and mark the cleat's position on the seat. Remove the back and fasten
the cleat in place, driving sixpenny nails through
the seat and into the braces. Replace the back
and nail it along the top to each wall stud and
along the bottom to the cleat.

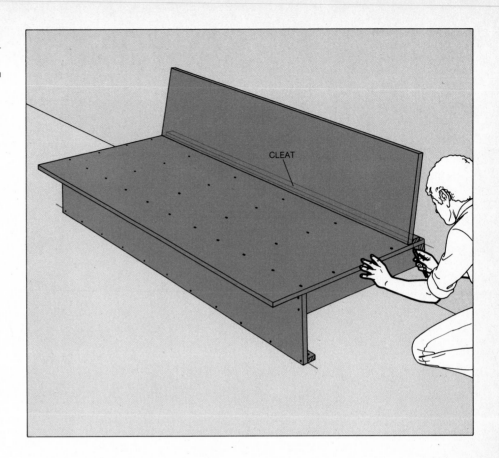

CLEAT

Adding an End Table

1 **The sofa side of the table.** Cut a plywood rectangle to extend from the wall to the back of the
kickboard and to rise as high as the table, less
¾ inch for the tabletop; nail this side of the table
to the seat frame and to the back every 6 inches.
If the height you have chosen sets the tabletop
below the top of the back, cut and fasten a plywood triangle to cover the back's open end.

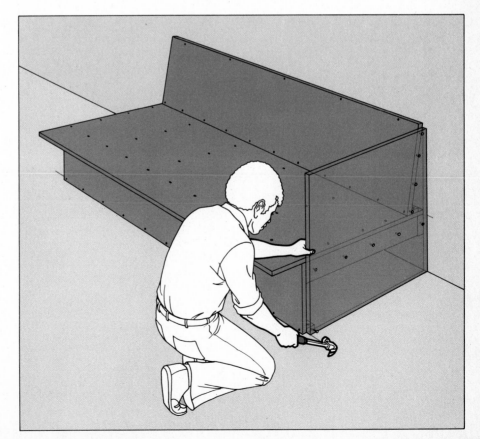

2 **Installing the cleats.** Using a tape measure and a level, draw two lines on the floor for the inside edges of the table front and outer side, and a third line on the wall for the vertical inside edge of this side; if your design permits, set the third line along the far side of a stud. At 6-inch intervals, nail 1-by-2 cleats directly inside of the floor lines. If the wall mark is aligned with a stud, nail the third cleat to the stud; otherwise, fasten this cleat to the wall with toggle bolts.

3 **Completing the table.** Cut the outer side of the table to match the side that fits against the end of the sofa, and nail it to the floor cleat. If the wall cleat at the back of the table area is nailed to a stud, nail the side to that cleat as well; if the wall cleat is toggle-bolted to the wall, fasten the side to the cleat with No. 10 screws. Cut and nail a front piece that will fit over the front edges of the sides. Cut and nail a top to fit over the sides and the front.

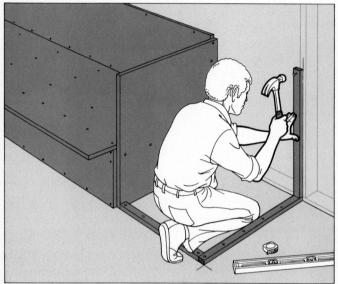

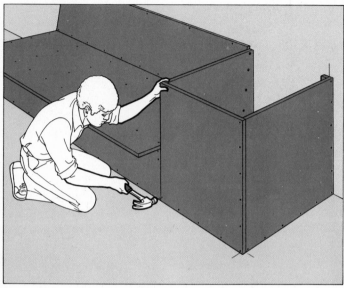

Connections at Corners

1 **Linking the frames.** Build a sofa frame with a level seat, butt one end into a corner and fasten the frame to the wall (*page 86, Step 3*). Build a second, similar frame with an extra interior brace 5¼ inches from the inner end, and install this frame with its end brace butted against the kickboard of the first; fasten the second frame to the first, driving nails through the end brace of the second frame and into the first frame's kickboard at 6-inch intervals.

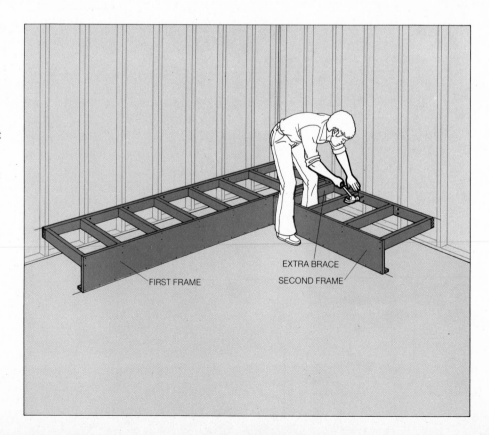

FIRST FRAME

EXTRA BRACE
SECOND FRAME

2 **Fitting the seats.** Install the seat of the first frame *(page 86, Step 3)* and nail the overlapping part of its overhang to the extra brace built into the second frame. For the second frame, cut a seat as deep as the seat of the first frame and wide enough to cover the exposed parts of the second frame; nail this seat to the extra brace and to the other parts of the frame.

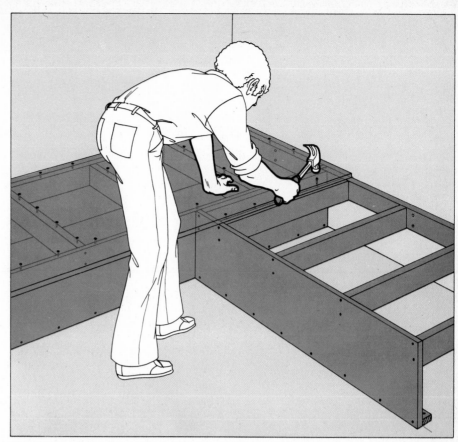

3 **Fitting the backs.** Install the back of the first frame to fit into the corner *(page 86, Steps 1 and 2)*, then butt a plywood sheet for the second back against the bottom of the first and, using a compass, scribe this sheet to fit against the first back. Cut the second back, at the scribed line, trim its other end flush with the outer end of the second frame, and nail it in place to the wall and to a cleat.

At each open end of the frames, build an end table *(pages 87-88, Steps 1-3)*.

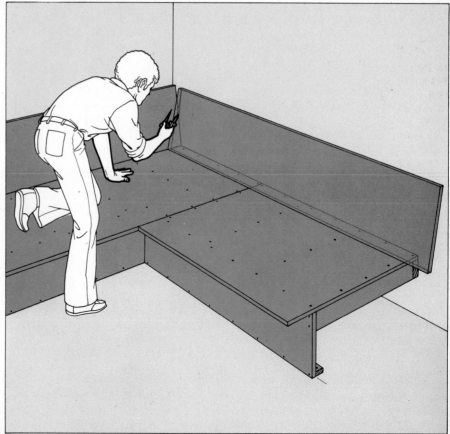

Beds Built in Layers, Horizontal or Vertical

In small or crowded rooms, freestanding beds squander valuable floor space and headroom—but the squandered space can be reclaimed or put to good use. A built-in bed that seems to vanish into a wall when not in use (opposite, top) saves floor space; a pair of bunk beds built in two tiers (below) uses the headroom. And an ordinary bed set into a built-in nook (opposite, bottom) uses its headroom to good effect—the curtained nook traps body heat and protects the bed from the drafts of a wintry bedroom.

The most dramatic space saver is the disappearing bed, which comes in twin (39 by 75 inches), full (54 by 75 inches) and queen (60 by 80 inches) sizes. The frame of the bed swings up from the floor into a simple wooden cabinet; the manufacturer supplies the frame and the hardware needed for its installation, but generally you must make the cabinet yourself (page 95). Many builders camouflage the cabinet, which juts about 2 feet into the room, with built-in shelving or cabinets on each side.

Two types of disappearing beds are available. The more elaborate and expensive has a plywood-panel bottom that rises with the bed; the panel comes in a variety of finishes, or can be finished to match the room around it. The simpler type has an exposed metal frame that must be hidden by cabinet doors.

A built-in bunk bed, like all built-ins, is fastened to the house frame. Because of this strong support, the frame can be made of ⁵⁄₄ lumber (which is slightly more than 1 inch thick) instead of heavy corner posts. Though the beds can be built to hold box springs and mattresses, most builders prefer to design them for shallower innerspring mattresses, which leave room for drawers and shelves. To increase headroom in rooms with low ceilings, use 6-inch sides rather than the 10-inch sides shown here.

The mattress for a manufactured bunk bed is 3 to 6 inches narrower than twin size; the length is the same. You may prefer to design your beds for conventional twin-sized mattresses, which cost about the same, are easier to fit with sheets and are generally better made.

A bunk bed. The floor, wall and ceiling provide solid support for this built-in bed; the bed itself can be assembled with thin boards and simple butt joints. Each of the posts at the corners consists of two butt-jointed ⁵⁄₄-inch boards, one an inch wider than the other so that the sides of the posts are the same width. Three tiers of 1-by-10 sides are screwed into the posts and to 1-by-4 spacers at the wall; the two lower tiers are fitted with 1-by-2 ledgers and ¾-inch plywood boards to hold the mattresses. Nailing blocks at the bottoms and tops of the posts are used to anchor the frame to the floor and ceiling.

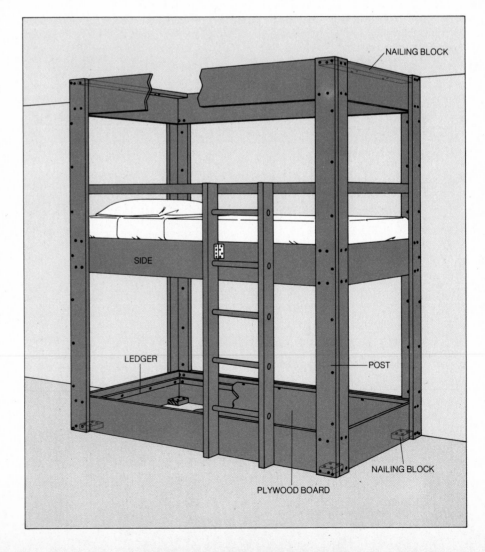

NAILING BLOCK

SIDE

LEDGER

POST

PLYWOOD BOARD

NAILING BLOCK

A bed that becomes a wall. This disappearing bed is built on a section of wall framing covered with a plywood panel. The frame is anchored to the floor with wood screws, driven through the bottom of a large cabinet. When the foot of the bed is lifted, spring-loaded hinges at the back of the frame help draw the bed into the closed position (*inset*), in which it is concealed behind the panel; handles on the panel are used to open the bed. The top of the frame is tapered to clear the top of the cabinet, and the mattress and box springs are strapped to the frame.

A bed that disappears behind doors. This bed is anchored and hinged like the one at left, but does not have a plywood panel covering the bottom. Instead, the bottom consists of an exposed metal frame that is concealed by a pair of cabinet doors when the bed is closed; the legs of the bed retract automatically as the bed is raised. Because the bed bottom is not a wall of the cabinet, the bed need not fit snugly in its cabinet—it can be installed in a cabinet large enough to include night tables, or in an existing closet with a wide opening.

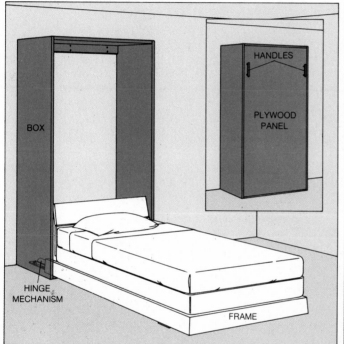

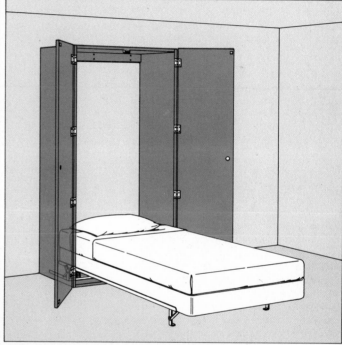

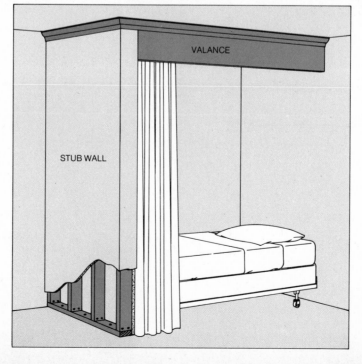

A bed in a built-in alcove. To create a niche for a bed in the corner of a room, a short wall called a stub wall is built of 2-by-4 studs and plates, and covered with wallboard. A curtain fitted with a valance conceals the bed by day and keeps off drafts at night; both the valance and the stub wall are capped with lengths of crown molding to fit them to the ceiling. The metal bedframe rolls out of the nook on casters when the bed is made up.

A Sturdy Double-decker

1 **Fastening posts to the wall.** At a corner of the bunk-bed location, countersink 3-inch No. 10 wood screws to fasten a 1-by-4, cut from $^{5}\!/_{4}$-inch stock to the height of the ceiling, to a wall stud at 12-inch intervals; then glue the outer edge of the board and screw a similar 1-by-5 to it at a right angle, using 2-inch No. 10 screws. Install the other wall post 71 inches away; if there is no stud at the second location, use toggle bolts to fasten the 1-by-4 to the wallboard.

Cut three 1-by-4 spacers to fit between the inner edges of the posts. Working at the stud locations, level and nail one spacer at the location you have chosen for the top of the lower bunk, generally about 10 inches above the floor; another at the top of the upper bunk, generally about 53 inches above the floor; and the third at the wall-ceiling corner.

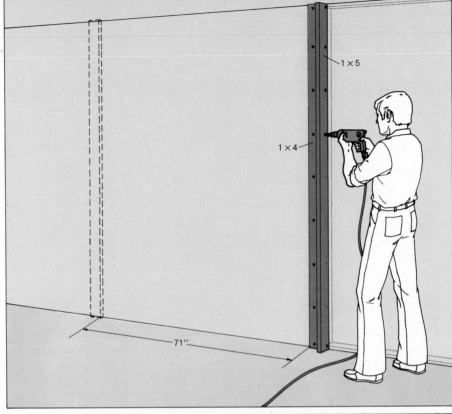

2 **Attaching sides to the wall.** Tack the top of a 1-by-10 board, cut to fit between the 1-by-5s in the wall posts, flush with the top of each spacer, and screw the board to the posts and the spacer with 3-inch No. 10 screws, countersinking four screws at each post and one at each stud.

For an end assembly, cut three 1-by-10 boards as wide as the mattress plus one inch—a total of 40 inches for a twin-sized mattress—then cut a 1-by-4 and 1-by-5 the height of the ceiling at the other end of the bed location and screw the 1-by-4 to the three sides.

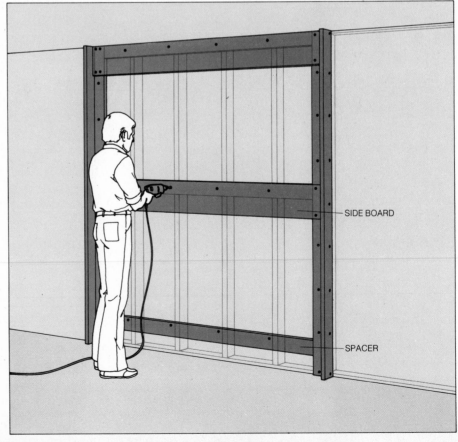

3 **Fastening the ends.** Tilt the end assembly
(Step 2, opposite, bottom) into place and fasten
its free ends at the inside corner of the wall
post. Screw a 1-by-5 onto the front edge of the
1-by-4; then cut, assemble and install an assembly for the other end of the bed.

Cut a 1-by-10 to the length of the wall sides
and fasten it loosely to the middle of the front
posts, using one screw at each post.

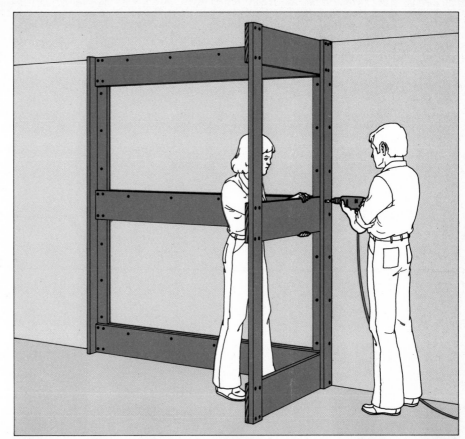

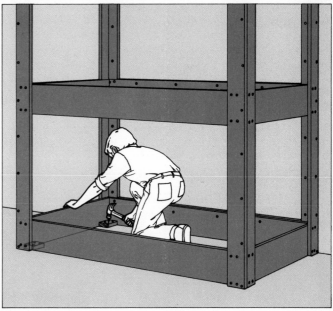

4 **Squaring the frame.** Measure the diagonals
between the inside corners of the posts at the
floor and ceiling. If the measurements differ,
adjust the frame by shifting the bases of the front
posts. When the frame is square and plumb,
mark the floor and ceiling at the inside corners of
the front posts and install all three sides at the
front posts. Be sure the posts are at their marks
as you work through Step 5.

5 **Securing the posts to the floor.** Set a block of
2-by-4 about 4 inches long at the inside corner of
each post, and nail it to the floor with four sixpenny nails. Nail the bottom of each front post to
its block from both sides with eightpenny finishing nails; nail the wall posts into their blocks
from the open sides. For a wall post set into a
corner, you need not use a nailing block; the fas-
tenings at the corner are adequate.

6 **Securing the posts to the ceiling.** Fit 2-by-4 blocks between the inside corners of the posts and at right angles to the joists above the ceiling, and, using eightpenny nails, fasten the blocks to the joists. Wherever possible, nail the outside face of each post to the end of a block.

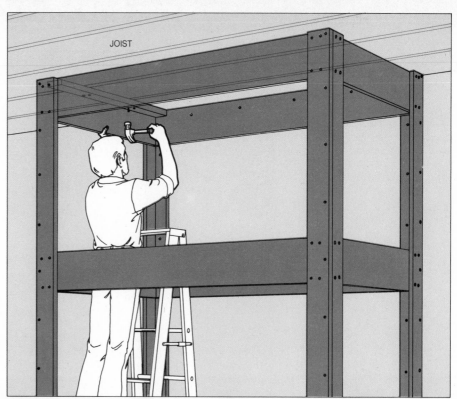

JOIST

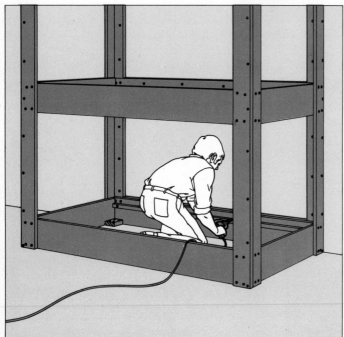

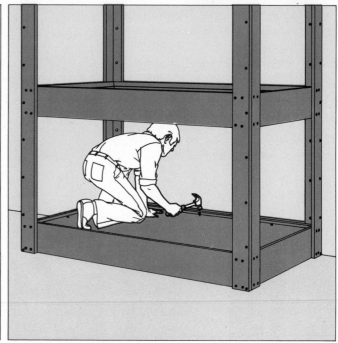

7 **Fastening ledgers.** At the bottom and middle tiers, screw a 1-by-2 ledger to a sidepiece between two inside corners, setting the ledger 1¾ inches from the top of the sidepiece and using 1½-inch No. 10 screws spaced at 12-inch intervals. Working around the tier, install three more ledgers in the same way, first fitting two ledgers between the end of one ledger and the next inside corner, then fitting the third between the ends of two ledgers.

8 **Nailing on a plywood foundation.** For each bunk, nail a ¾-inch plywood board, cut to the inside dimensions of the sides, onto the ledgers, using fourpenny nails at 12-inch intervals. Mat-tresses can be set directly on these boards.

Install a ladder (*page 118, center*) at one end of the bunk beds. As guardrails for the open sides of the upper bunk, nail 1-by-3s between the insides of the posts 6 inches above the mattress.

A Bed that Flips into a Wall

1 **Making the cabinet.** Build a four-sided ¾-inch
plywood cabinet, open on both sides. Butt-nail the
sides to the top and bottom and fasten a 1-by-4
cleat between the sides at the top rear; drive the
nails for the cleat through the sides and top. A
cabinet for a bed with a paneled bottom must fit
the panel precisely, and the manufacturer will
prescribe its dimensions; for a bed with a metal-
frame bottom, the cabinet need only be larger
than the frame. Tilt the box up against the wall.

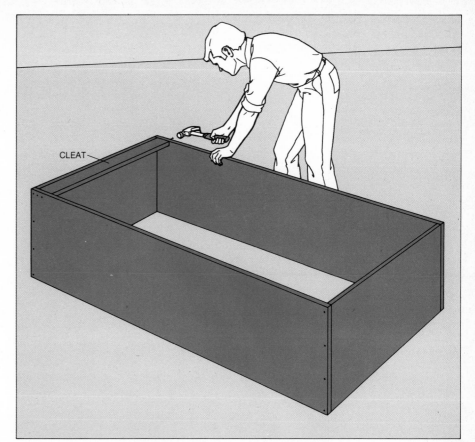

CLEAT

2 **Securing the cabinet.** Nail the cabinet to the wall
studs through the cleat, using two eightpenny
nails at each stud; nail it to the floor through the
bottom, using sixpenny nails at 12-inch intervals. Fasten the end of the bed to the cabinet according to the manufacturer's instructions. If
the bed has a metal-frame bottom, add doors to
the box (*pages 36-37*), preferably secured
with magnetic catches (*page 41, bottom*). A bed
with a paneled bottom needs no doors, but the
panel should be finished to match or complement
the walls of the room.

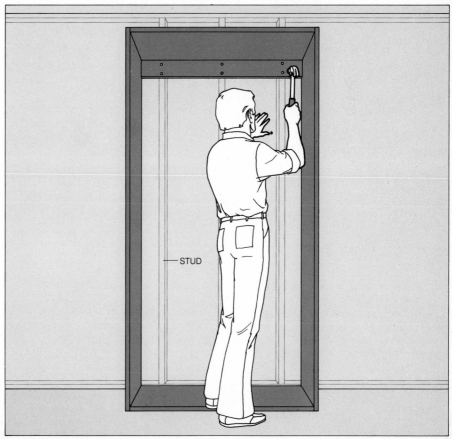

STUD

How to Build Tables that Hang from the Walls

A built-in table—or its higher, narrower cousin, the snack counter—is the most convenient furnishing for informal family meals. It can be designed to fill a space precisely—or to fill no space at all when not in use—and it is assembled, quickly and inexpensively, on the spot. It does not have to be in the kitchen, for it adds great convenience to a bedroom, recrea-

tion room or breakfast nook, and can convert a living-room corner into a dining area. A counter, generally 36 inches high, might be as long as a room; a table, generally 6 inches lower, can run as far along or out from the wall as its bench or pair of benches, and fit to any width between a bench and a wall or between two benches, so long as its edge is

about even with the edge of the seats.

Stationary tabletops, fixed to a wall, are the simplest to build. One that fills an alcove can rest on wall cleats. When extended from a single wall, a table needs stronger support—a triangular bracket for a table extending up to 26 inches, one or more legs for longer tables.

A folding table, trickier to build, disap-

Three Designs for Stationary Tables

Cleats for an alcove table. L-shaped cleats, screwed to the studs behind the walls, support a tabletop set into a nook, as shown here, or into a corner, with the free end of the table supported by a leg. The cleats are made of 1-by-2s; they are assembled with screws driven at 12-inch intervals before being fastened to the wall. The tabletop is secured by screws driven up through the projecting pieces of the cleats.

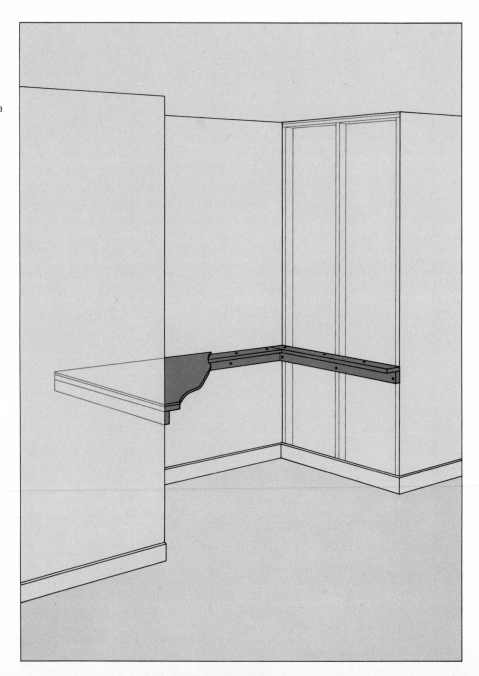

pears into a wall opening or a wall-mounted cabinet, so that it occupies no floor space when not needed. In a non-bearing wall, the opening can be any width; in a bearing wall, do not cut more than one stud. Where a wall recess is not practical—in a masonry wall, for example, or in a stud wall that contains insulation, ducts or pipes—build a backless cabinet (pages 8-10) 3½ inches deep for the tables shown on these pages, and fasten it to the wall with L braces.

For strength and rigidity, the top of a folding table is generally fitted with a piano hinge (page 99, top); the legs are usually fitted with T hinges and stiffened by folding braces. A table that swings up to close must have a top at least as long as the legs, so that the legs will fit in the recess or cabinet.

A gate-leg table also uses a piano hinge, but closes down rather than up; its legs, hinged to the sides of a recess or cabinet that rises from the floor, slide back and are concealed by the tabletop.

The tops for built-in tables are generally made of ¾-inch plywood; a surface of plastic laminate may be preferable in some situations for its resistance to liquids and stains, and a full-sized flush door up to 1¾ inches thick can be used for a large stationary table. Legs for folding tables are generally 2-by-2s; for stationary tables, ½- to ¾-inch plywood—but prefabricated designs in shaped wooden and metal legs are also available.

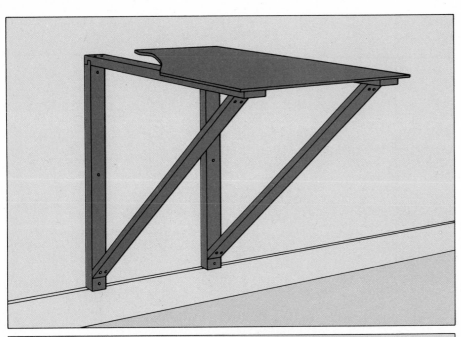

Brackets for a cantilevered table. A top extending as much as 26 inches out from a wall is supported by triangular 2-by-4 brackets. The vertical legs of the triangles rise from the baseboard and are screwed to the studs behind the wall at top, bottom and center. The horizontal legs, cut 2 inches shorter than the depth of the table, are dadoed to receive the ends of rabbets on the vertical legs beneath them, and are fastened to these legs with glue and screws.

The diagonal legs, bevel-cut at top and bottom, are fastened to the other legs with screws driven through deeply counterbored pilot holes; the ends of the diagonal braces are set 1 inch in from the ends of the others, leaving room for a screw driven through the outer end of the horizontal leg into the tabletop, and for a screw through the bottom of the vertical leg into a stud.

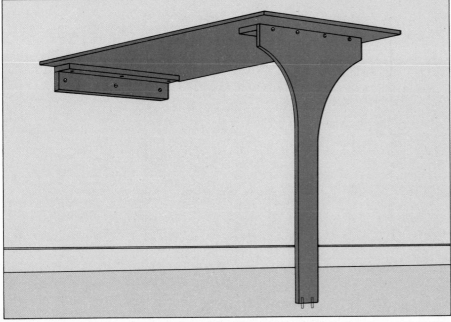

A panel leg for the end of a table. A top extending more than 26 inches out from a wall is supported at its inner end by an L-shaped cleat (opposite) and at its outer end by a plywood panel leg, tapered so it will give firm support at the top and easy access under the table at the bottom. The leg, made of plywood at least ½ inch thick, is fastened to the floor with two dowels, 2 inches long, glued into floor and leg holes made with the aid of a doweling jig (page 33); its top is screwed to a 1-by-2 cleat, and the cleat is screwed to the tabletop.

Recesses for Hinged Tables

Anatomy of a recess. Cut into a bearing wall, this recess for a drop-down table consists of a rectangular opening strengthened by a framing of 2-by-4s—a header, a sill and stud segments. The header and sill are two 2-by-4s set on edge and separated by ½-inch plywood spacers; they are toenailed to the studs at the sides of the opening and to the cut studs above and below it. Segments are face-nailed to the side studs.

A ½-inch plywood sheet is glued to the wallboard at the back of the recess, and plywood facing boards are glued and nailed to the sides, top and bottom of the new framing, flush with the finish wall. Lengths of doorstop, or stop molding, nailed ½ inch from the front edges of the side and top facing boards, fit the recess for ½-inch doors. Scraps of the wallboard cut away for the recess cover the new framing, and lengths of miter-cut molding trim the opening.

A recess for a gate-leg table (*page 100*) is framed without a sill (*inset*). Here, the stud segments are jack studs, resting on the sole plate; between them, the sole plate is cut away, and a strip of ¾-inch plywood brings the bottom of the recess flush with the floor. No trim is used: the table-top hides the edges of the opening.

A recess in a nonbearing wall is framed more lightly and without stud segments. For the header and sill, single 2-by-4s are set flat and nailed to the cut studs and side studs.

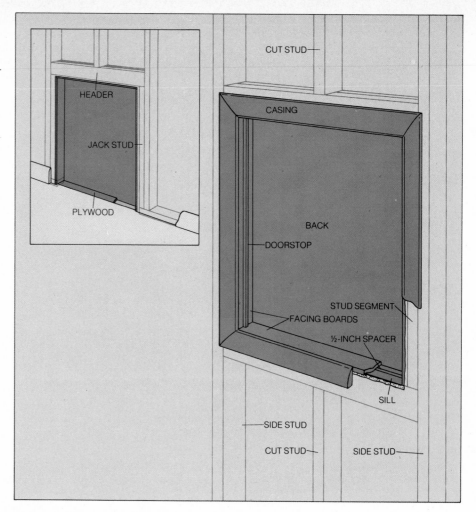

A Table to Fold Down from a Wall Recess

1 Attaching the legs. With the tabletop upside down, use a 3-inch T hinge to fasten each leg to the top, 2 inches in from the edges of a corner. The crosspiece of the hinge is screwed to the table and the strap is screwed to the leg.

2 **Hinging the top.** Use a piano hinge to fasten the tabletop into the recess, screwing one leaf of the hinge to the tabletop and the other to the recess back. Close the hinged top into the recess, install a sliding bolt at the upper edge of the underside of the tabletop and drill a hole through the top facing board to accept the bolt (*inset*).

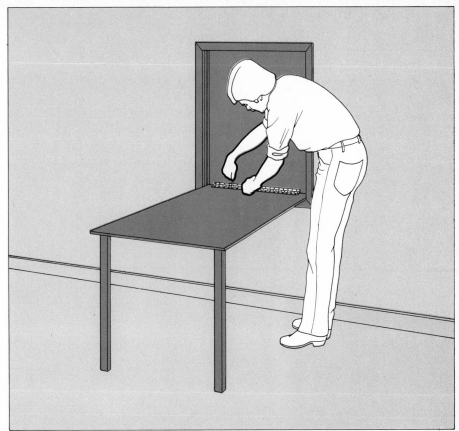

3 **Bracing the legs.** Open the table, plumb the right leg with a level, and screw a right-hand folding brace to the outside of the leg and to the underside of the tabletop. Attach a left-hand brace to the other leg.

With the table closed, fit the recess with cabinet doors (*pages 37-40*) and use magnetic catches at the top of the recess (*page 41*).

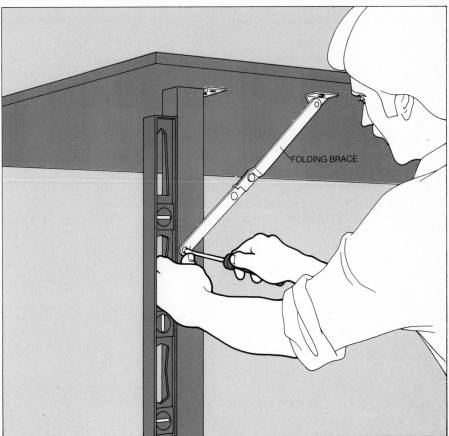

FOLDING BRACE

A Gate-leg Table to Lift Up

Anatomy of a gate-leg table. A horizontal piano hinge secures the inner end of this table to the top facing board of a recess. The 2-by-2 legs supporting the outer end are mortised to the rails, which are hinged vertically to the sides of the recess. When the leg-and-rail assemblies are swung out, they are held in place by wedge-shaped blocks on the underside of the table. A slight tap will release the legs from the blocks; the leg-and-rail assemblies can then be folded back into the recess, and the tabletop folded down, covering the wall opening and its contents.

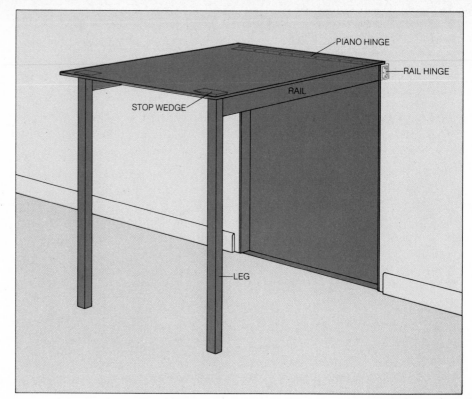

Building the Table

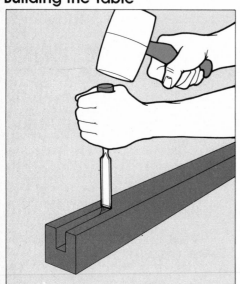

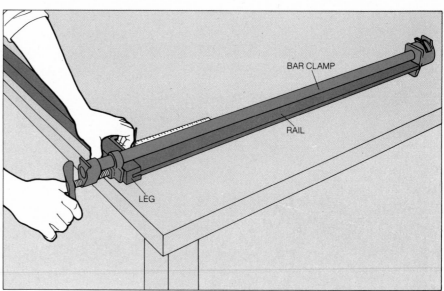

1 **Mortising the legs.** Make 2-by-2 legs ⅜ inch shorter than the height of the table recess; in one end of each, make a mortise ⅜ inch wide, 1 inch deep and 3 inches long (*page 38*). Square the round ends of the mortises with a mortising chisel and mallet.

Cut two ¾-by-3-inch rails to match the width of the recess. On one end of each, make a tenon (*page 39*) ⅜ inch thick and 1 inch long to fit the mortises.

2 **The leg-and-rail assemblies.** Glue each leg and rail together and secure the assembly in a bar clamp, using a combination square as you tighten the clamp to make sure the joint stays square.

When the glue is dry, remove the assemblies from the clamps and trim each to its final length. Cut one rail so its length—from the outside of the leg to the hinge end of the rail—is 1 inch shorter than the recess width; cut the other shorter than the first by the thickness of the leg.

3 **Hinging the rails.** Set the longer leg-and-rail assembly at the back of the recess, check that the rail is level and parallel to the back, and fasten the rail to the facing board at the side of the recess with a 3-inch butt hinge. Set the shorter assembly in place against the first and hinge it to the opposite side of the recess.

Make a tabletop as long as the recess is high and wide enough to overlap the recess sides.

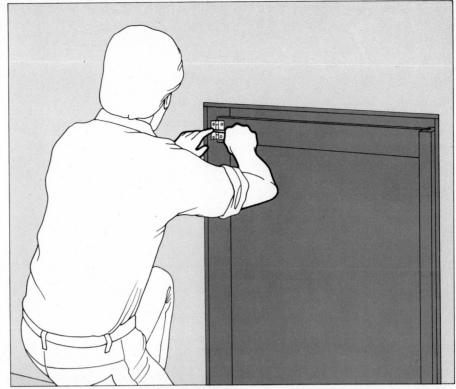

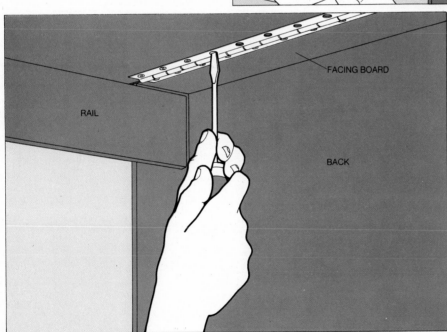

RAIL

FACING BOARD

BACK

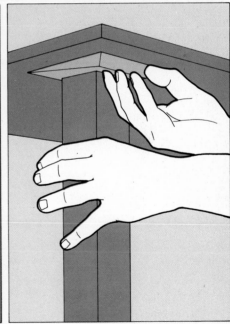

4 **Hinging the top.** Lay the tabletop on the extended leg-and-rail assemblies and secure it to the top facing board of the recess with a piano hinge, aligning the hinge pin with the line between the tabletop and the facing board.

5 **Making stops for the legs.** Check to be sure that the assemblies are perpendicular to the wall, then mark the outlines of the legs on the underside of the tabletop to position the stop wedges. Test-fit, then glue stop blocks, cut from 4-inch lengths of 1-by-3, to the underside of the table, setting the thick end of each block just inside the outline of the leg position with the cut side against the table. Swing the leg against the wedge to hold it firmly, and rest a heavy object on the tabletop until the glue dries.

3

Platforms that Remake a Room

A lofty bedroom. A sleeping loft like the one at left, photographed just before completion, can make a room of even modest proportions do double duty. The loft, an elevated platform with a protective rail, provides just enough floor space for a bed and just enough headroom to permit sitting up; the limited space beneath becomes storage or a study. The ship's ladder will be secured to the platform with the framing connectors lying on the top step.

When the ancient Greeks devised the amphitheater of terraced seats surrounding a raised stage, they introduced a design concept that architects have been exploiting ever since: the use of changes in floor and seating levels to create a dramatic effect. A dining area elevated above the floor of the room on a low platform becomes a special place for meals. A depressed section of floor, defined by an enclosing platform for seating—the conversation pit—establishes a friendly environment for socializing. A balcony-like platform on pillars—the loft—makes an appealing sanctum that paradoxically is partially private and partially on view.

Each one of these applications of raised floor sections serves a practical function beyond drama, and practical platforms can be spectacular when several are combined in a large room *(pages 67 and 69):* They divide living space into areas suited for specific purposes—eating, conversing, sleeping, working.

Although lofts, conversation pits and step-up dining areas look different, all are basically one simple kind of built-in, the platform, and their construction is straightforward carpentry. Yet they represent such substantial modifications in the design and traffic patterns of the house that they must be well planned. In addition to allowing for family traffic patterns and the location of doors and windows, you may also need to modify heating, cooling and electrical installations before beginning construction. A raised platform such as that defining a conversation pit often blocks heating outlets or radiators. A section of wallboard will have to be removed so that wall ducts can be extended up to the level of the rim. Similarly, vertical extensions for baseboard heaters—either pipes or wires—must be installed before the pit is assembled so that the heating units can be remounted at points along the walls where they will be the most effective.

Since heat rises, heating a loft is rarely a problem, but the ducts for air conditioning should be extended at least a foot above the platform of the loft, either inside the wall or through an extended floor duct enclosed in a wallboard-covered frame. To bring cool air up to a sleeping platform, a simple air siphon—a length of ducting with a fan attachment to circulate air—may be enough. Electrical outlets may also have to be extended upward so that they are situated above lofts and conversation pits.

Before you begin construction, consider how you intend to carry the large framing members into the room, where you will stack them, and how you will move them into place without damaging the room. Remember that a substantial stock of big boards will be needed, and it is easy to pack the room with so many building materials that there is barely space to wield a hammer.

An Elevated Floor for Dining or Lounging

Platforms built with the solidity and permanence of the floor below them offer attractive alternatives to walls and furniture as a way to organize space. They landscape interiors the way hills and valleys set apart sections of the outdoors.

A low dining platform, for example, defines and dramatizes an eating area without dividing a room into cramped cubicles. In multiple levels, platforms alter a room's original contours while creating new seating and lounging areas; in their most familiar form—a conversation pit softened with carpeting and cushions—multilevel platforms take the place of conventional couches and chairs.

Like any large, permanent structure, a platform must be carefully planned. Begin by measuring the ceiling height—though stacked platforms can rise to any height, you need a minimum ceiling height of 6 feet above the highest.

From this point on, most of your planning can be done on a sketch of the room, on which you indicate the locations of doors, windows, registers and electrical outlets. Add the platform's outline, and consider the effect of the structure on traffic patterns; if the platform

will block any utility outlets, plan their relocation or change the platform design.

Now add the location of each floor joist that runs below the platform. Find the joists by inspecting the basement or by drilling small holes in the floor and probing with a stiff wire. Their location is important because the new joists that support the platform floor must lie directly over the old joists.

On your drawing, specify exact dimensions for the front and back of a ¾-inch plywood platform frame parallel to—but not necessarily over—the floor joists. Add ¾-inch plywood sides and plywood dividers parallel to the sides and no more than 6 feet apart; if the platform runs two thirds the length of the floor joists, use at least two dividers. Finally, indicate the positions of 2-by-4 platform joists running between the sides and dividers and over the floor joists.

Cut and assemble this basic structure by the method on these pages and, if you wish, complete the platform with carpeting (pages 109-111). To create a multilevel platform, combine simple rectangular platforms for the shape you want. The top of a lower platform can double as a

step up to a higher one, or you can stack ¾-inch plywood boxes as separate steps. A step should be no more than 8 inches high, and its tread depth plus its riser height should equal 18 inches: for example, a riser 8 inches high needs a 10-inch tread; a 4-inch riser, a 14-inch tread.

The top of a lower platform can also double as a seat, the frame of a platform above serving as a back rest. A seat that simply will be carpeted should be 14 to 16 inches high and 24 to 26 inches deep; a back 14 to 16 inches high is standard. Cushioned seats can be 8 to 14 inches off the floor, the cushions bringing the height up to 16 inches; set the back of a cushioned seat 30 to 32 inches from the front. The front edge of the platform seat should overhang the frame by 4 inches to create heel space.

Draw the outline of an upper-level platform over that of the platform below, aligning its dividers and joists with those of the lower platform. If the side of an upper platform does not rest on the side of the lower one, add an extra divider to the lower platform at this location; if the front or back of the platforms does not align, add extra joists to the lower one.

Anatomy of a platform. This single-level platform has a frame built of ¾-inch plywood, with its front and back running parallel to the floor joists of the room; the sides of the frame and the dividers within it run perpendicular to the joists. Frame sections longer than 8 feet are spliced together with truss plates. The plywood floor of the platform is supported by the frame, the dividers, 2-by-4 joists nailed between the sides and the dividers, and blocking nailed between the joists. Anchors made of 2-by-4 blocks carry the weight of each platform joist to a room joist below it, level the platform and secure the frame to the floor.

At the wall, the platform is lag-bolted to the studs of the room. Shimmed spacers inserted between the frame and the wall at the lag-bolt locations make a snug fit above the baseboard, which is left in place for this installation. The gaps between the corners of the frame and the wall above the baseboard are closed by filler strips, which provide nailing surfaces for the carpet and padding that cover the platform.

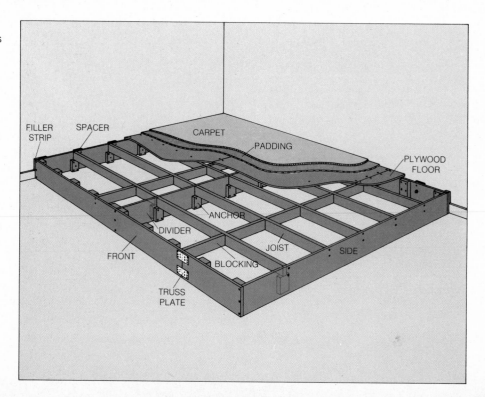

FILLER STRIP · SPACER · CARPET · PADDING · PLYWOOD FLOOR · ANCHOR · DIVIDER · JOIST · SIDE · FRONT · BLOCKING · TRUSS PLATE

Building a Platform

1 Laying out the frame. After arranging the parts of the frame—front, back, sides and divider—on the floor near its final location, make frame sections longer than 8 feet by butting lengths of plywood together and nailing truss plates at the top and bottom of each side of the joint. Stagger these truss joints at the front and back or at opposite sides of the frame.

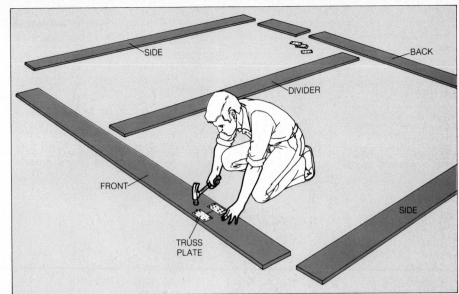

2 Putting the frame together. Sink self-tapping, 1⅝-inch No. 6 Phillips dry-wall screws through the front and back frame pieces into the ends of each side and divider, using a ⅜-inch variable-speed electric drill and a No. 1 Phillips screwdriver bit. Drive screws 1 inch from the top and bottom of the frame; space additional screws between them, no more than 8 inches apart.

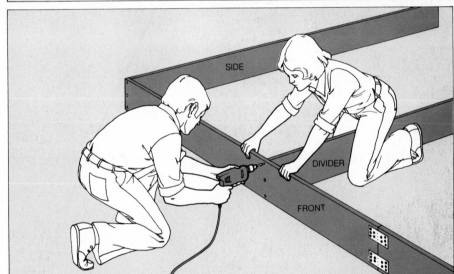

3 Installing the joists. Face-nail 2-by-4 joists between the sides and dividers, flush with the top of the frame and spaced to be directly over the joists below the floor of the room when the platform is in its final position. Where joists meet on each side of a divider, butt-nail one joist and drive the nails at an angle through the divider and into the end of the other (*inset*).

As you install the joists and again after you have moved the frame into position, check the frame for squareness by measuring diagonally across the top in both directions; if necessary, shift the frame by pushing or hammering it until the measurements are equal.

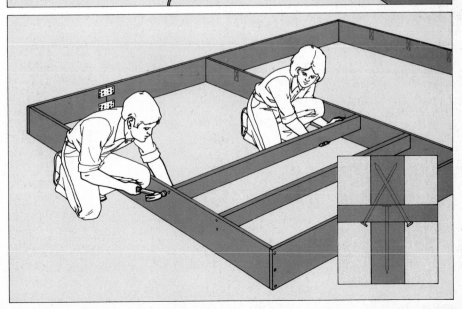

4 Leveling the frame. Check the frame on all four sides with a carpenter's level and insert shims—the cedar shingles used to shim door and window frames will do—underneath its edges to level the entire assembly.

SHIMS

5 Fastening the frame to a wall. Locate the studs alongside the platform, fill the gap between the frame and the wall at each stud location with shingle shims and drive a nail through the frame, shims and wall into the stud. Drill a pilot hole and screw a ¼-inch lag bolt 3 inches long through the frame into the stud. At each gap between the wall and the corner of the frame above the baseboard, snugly fit a filler strip made of layers of plywood 2 inches wide, and drive nails through the frame and the filler strip into the wall.

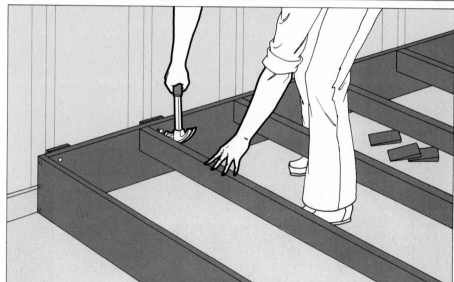

6 Anchoring the platform. Stand a 2-by-4 beside each end of each platform joist, mark it at the bottom of the joist and cut it at the mark. Set the cut piece, called an anchor, under the end of the joist and nail it to the side or divider; toe-nail it to the floor. Fit additional anchors flush with the top of the front and back of the frame where they meet the sides and dividers and at 16-inch intervals between these points; screw these anchors to the frame with 2⅛-inch No. 6 self-tapping dry-wall screws, driven in pairs at 3-inch intervals along the anchor.

Remove the shims under the frame and check for gaps greater than ½ inch between the floor and frame sections. If you plan to cover the entire platform with carpeting, face these sections with ¼-inch plywood scribed to the floor and cut flush with the top of the frame.

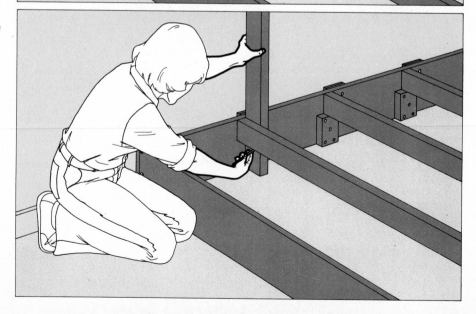

7 **Fitting the platform floor.** Lay a plywood panel across the joists and use a carpenter's square
to align its edges parallel to the frame. If the
platform fits into a corner, start fitting the floor
from that point; if there is any gap of more
than ½ inch between the edge of the plywood and
the wall, scribe the sheet to fit (page 48, bottom). At the last joist completely covered by the
panel, trim the plywood edge to cover ¾ inch
of the joist. Where an edge crosses joists, center
2-by-4 blocking between the joists to support
the edge when the floor is installed.

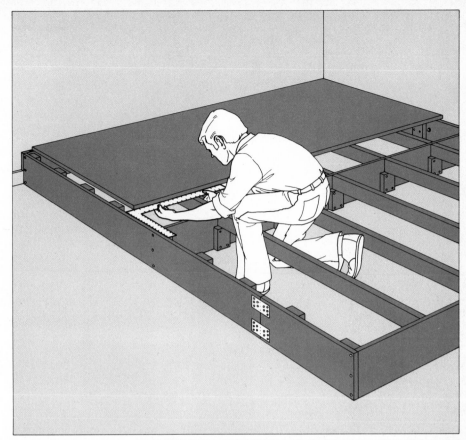

8 **Nailing the floor in place.** Run ¼-inch beads of
subfloor construction adhesive in zigzag patterns along the tops of the joists, frame and dividers with a caulking gun. Fasten a plywood
panel to the edges of the frame with 1⅝-inch
No. 6 self-tapping dry-wall screws at 6-inch
intervals. Nail the edges of the panel to the blocking and joists at 6-inch intervals; nail it to the
other joists below it at 10-inch intervals.

Install the other sections of the floor with a
⅛-inch gap between panels. Trim panels that
overhang the platform flush with the frame.

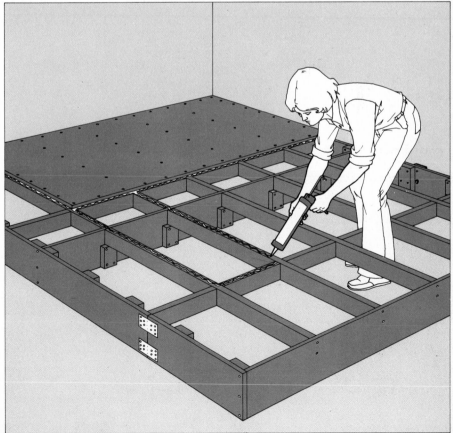

Platforms as Furniture

A conversation pit. In this typical arrangement, six simple platforms are stacked to form a U of seating around a fireplace. Three platforms, 8 inches high, rest on the floor—a main platform (top drawing, foreground) flanked by two smaller wings. They are built by modifying the method described on pages 104-107 to omit joists and anchors in the areas that will lie directly under the upper-level platform when the pit is completed (bottom drawing). In the wings, dividers are located to support the sides of the upper wings—if necessary, extra dividers would be installed for this purpose—and cleats are fastened to the dividers as nailing surfaces for plywood seats. In the main platform, joists are located to support the front and back of the upper main platform, and blocking provides nailing surfaces for the main-platform seats.

In the platforms for the upper level, each 16 inches high, anchors rise from the floor to the bottoms of joists and the tops of the frames; the joists support the plywood tops of the upper level. On the lower level, plywood sheets have been installed over the exposed parts of the base platforms. In the seating area, these sheets overhang the platform frames by 4 inches to provide heel space; at the outer edge of the main platform, they fit flush with the frame. A plywood box 8 inches high provides an intermediate step between the upper and lower levels of the main platform; an identical box (not shown) serves the same purpose in the seating area.

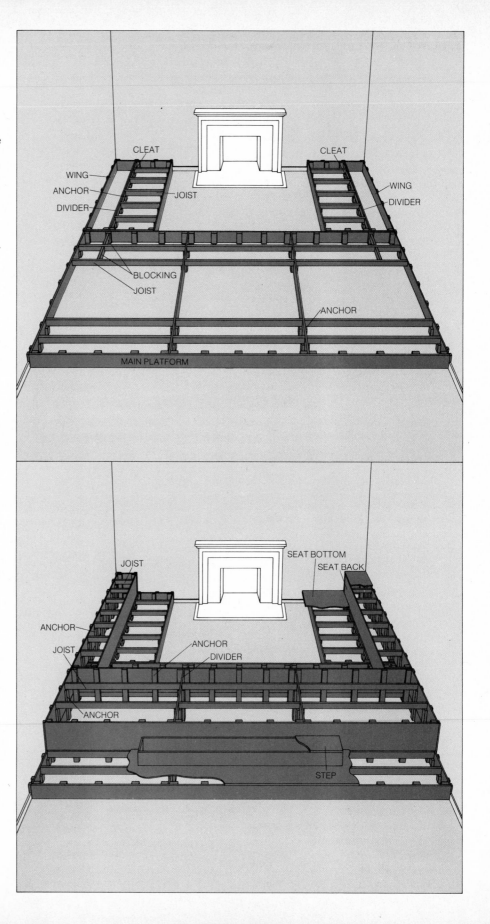

Carpeting for Comfort

A layer of carpeting makes a plywood platform complete. The carpet and its padding cover the rough edges, muffle footsteps that would otherwise reverberate in the hollow platform, and make an inviting surface on which to sit or recline.

Almost any jute-backed carpeting can be used if installed over padding, though shag styles are a poor choice for a platform with steps—the sparse pile does not wear well. The best padding for a platform is "scrim-faced" latex foam.

You will need about 2 per cent more padding than the square footage of the platform top and sides. Buy enough carpeting to cover the platform completely, allowing an extra 3 inches in each direction for trimming. The pile direction, which runs with the length of the carpet as it comes off its original roll, will determine the alignment of the carpet along the platform: The pile should run down the "main edge"—that is, the edge most often used to step onto the platform.

If the platform is too large to be covered by a single width of carpeting, you must plan to seam pieces together with a type of fabric tape, coated with hot-melt adhesive, used by carpet layers. Melt the adhesive with a special seaming iron available from agencies that rent carpeting tools. The pile must run in the same direction on both sides of the seam.

The carpet is held to the floor by stretching it over a gripping "tackless" strip—a plywood strip with projecting pinpoints—which is nailed around the perimeter of the platform, pinpoints up. Buy strip with pins long enough to grip the back of the carpet you have chosen, but not so long that you can feel them through the face. You will also need an awl, to stretch carpeting along a tackless strip; and a specialized tool, available at rental agencies, called a knee-kicker—a telescoping shaft that hooks an end of the carpet so that you can stretch carpeting to a strip by repeatedly kicking the tool with your knee.

The platform shown here, like the example on page 104, is enclosed by walls on two adjacent sides, but you can carpet any platform by the same procedures. Stretch the carpeting along two sides first, leaving about 6 inches at each end unfastened. To stretch the remaining sides, start each at the end of one of the first two.

To carpet a conversation-pit seat, which overhangs the frame, fasten the carpet with tacks at the front of the seat, fold it under the overhang and fasten it there with tacks or carpet adhesive. Use a separate strip of carpeting for the platform sides underneath the overhang.

Whatever the configuration of your platform, prepare it for the carpeting job in the same way. On the free sides, round the vertical and the top-to-side corners with a rasp or a router. Then, before installing tackless strip, sweep the platform and the room thoroughly.

Laying the Carpet

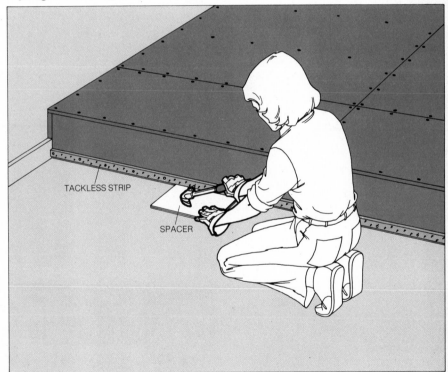

1 Installing tackless strip. Wearing gloves, nail tackless strip along the bottom of the platform and along the top next to the walls. Position the strip with its angled pins pointing away from the area to be carpeted, and with a gap two thirds the thickness of the carpet between the strips and the wall or floor. To set the gap, use a spacer made of layers of cardboard glued together; flex the strip to keep the gap constant along an uneven floor or wall. Cut the strip 1½ inches short of each outside corner and, on a platform with a step, 1½ inches short of outside corners formed by the intersection of the platform and the step.

On a step, install the tackless strip as you would on a platform, but set the strips at the back of the tread and the side of the platform to leave a gap of ⅝ inch between them, with the pins of the strips pointing toward each other. To carpet a room and platform at the same time, join the room and platform carpet as you would the sections of carpet on a stair tread and platform side (*page 111*).

2 **Laying padding.** Within the area bounded by the tackless strips, lay widths of padding, fabric side up, to overlap the strips; staple the edges of each piece to the platform at 6-inch intervals, and use a utility knife held at a 45° angle to trim the padding to a beveled edge even with the inner edge of the strips. Trim padding flush to walls and baseboards beside the platform, then seal padding seams with duct tape. At the top of an outside corner, trim each piece of padding away from the corner at a 45° angle to a point 1½ inches from the corner, then cut straight down to the floor *(inset)*; at the inside corner of a step, trim the padding back 1½ inches.

Arrange the carpet on the platform with its pile pointing down the main edge and at least ⅜ inch of overlap along the floor and walls. Cut the edges of the carpet to make it lie flat.

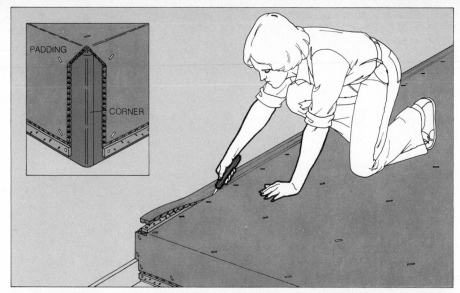

3 **Stretching carpet along the main edge.** At one end of the main platform edge, press the carpet onto the pins of the tackless strip with the face of a hammer, and stay-tack the carpet to the strip with a carpet tack driven partway in; then, at the other end of the main edge, push the point of an awl through the carpet and into the tackless strip. Use the awl to pry the carpet edge sideways along the strip, stretching it taut, then press the carpet onto the tackless strip and stay-tack it 6 inches from the end. Working between the stay tacks, press the carpet edge onto the tackless strip, and secure it with strips of wood tacked over the strips. Stretch the adjacent edge of the carpet, starting at the corner and working toward the wall.

On a main edge with a step, cut the carpet roughly around the step, then stretch from the wall to the step, along the tread of the step and from the step to the corner, driving stay tacks at the beginning and end of each stretch.

4 **Using the knee-kicker.** Starting at a wall and working on hands and knees, hold a carpet knee-kicker, adjusted to the carpet thickness, with the hand that is closer to the corner of the room. Set the knee-kicker at a 45° angle to the wall and pointing into the corner, position the head of the kicker about an inch from the wall, and kick the pad of the tool with the knee that is closer to the corner, to stretch the carpet and hook it onto the tackless strip. Move along the wall, hooking the carpet as you go and holding it hooked with your free hand. Repeat the procedure on the adjacent wall, then trim the carpet to an overlap of ⅜ inch up the wall. Tuck the overlap into the gap between the wall and the tackless strip with a screwdriver blade.

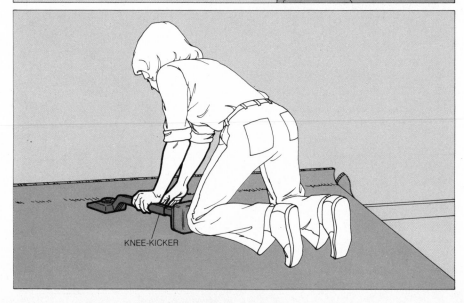

5 **Fitting the carpet to an outside corner.** Starting an inch from the platform, slit the carpet diagonally away from the corner; continue the slit back upward to the rounded top of the corner, and fold the triangular waste pieces back. Trim these flaps so that 1¼ inches will project beyond the corner, and trim 3 inches along the bottom of each flap flush with the floor. Turn the flaps under to the best-looking fit, then stay-tack them in place.

6 **Stitching the corner.** Thread a curved carpet needle with No. 18 linen carpet thread coated with beeswax, make a large knot in the long end and, starting at the back of the carpet, loop the needle through a folded edge of the carpet at the top of the corner. Pull the thread through, loop the needle into the carpet edge opposite this stitch, and guide the needle inside the carpet to bring it out ½ to ¾ inch below the entry point; then pull the thread taut.

Continue this over-and-down pattern to the bottom of the corner. There, drive a tack partway and loop the thread around it a few times; then, drive the tack all the way in and snip off the excess thread *(inset)*.

Trim the carpet flush with the walls and baseboards beside the platform. Remove the stay tacks from the carpet and the wood strips holding the carpet down over the tackless strip.

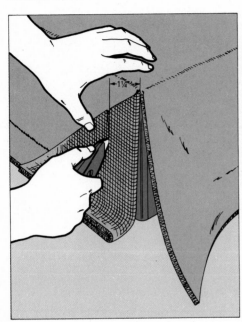

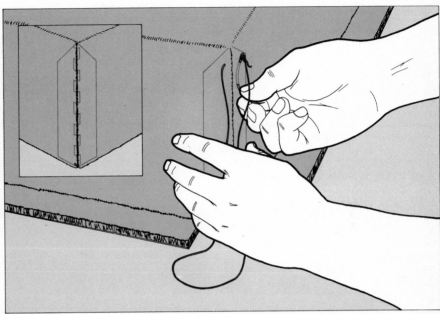

Covering a Step

Stretching the carpet. Lay the carpet with its pile pointing down the step and press it onto a tackless strip at the bottom of the riser, then use a knee-kicker angled away from the center of the step to stretch it onto a tackless strip at the back of the tread. Trim the waste above the step with a utility knife held on its side on the tread, then tuck the remainder into the space behind the tackless strip with a carpet installer's stair tool or a wide, dull cold chisel.

Use the knee-kicker to stretch the carpet down the sides of the step onto the middle of a tackless strip at the bottom of each side and stay-tack it. Trim and sew the outside corners *(Steps 5 and 6, above)*; finish the back corners by trimming the carpet, turning it under and tacking the flaps with 24-ounce tacks. Stretch the carpet onto the remainder of the tackless strip on each side and remove the stay tacks.

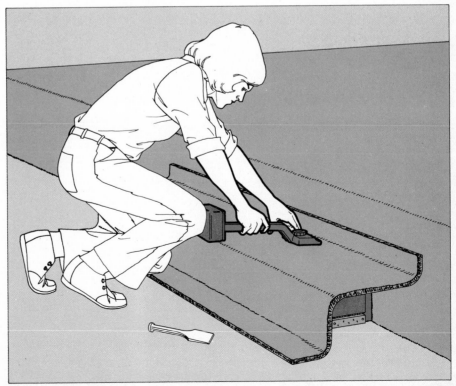

The Loft: A Balcony to Stretch a Room

In an older home with high ceilings, you can build in extra living space with a loft, or balcony, that provides a sleeping platform or even an entire extra room. For a complete second-story room, you should have a ceiling at least 15 feet high—most building codes require an average height of 7½ feet in any living space. However, a small sleeping platform with about 4 feet above it—enough for an adult to sit on the bed—can be built into a room that has a ceiling as low as 10 feet; you can use the space under the platform for chests or a desk.

The materials for loft-building are standard: structural-grade joists, plywood, construction adhesive applied with a caulking gun, and ¾-inch finish boards to cover exposed edges of the loft frame. The maximum spans for joists spaced at 16-inch intervals and carrying a load of 40 pounds per square foot (strong enough for a roomful of people) are: 2-by-6s—9 feet; 2-by-8s—12 feet; 2-by-10s—15 feet. Building methods are straightforward but you will need helpers for some steps of the job, such as lifting the frame for a sleeping platform into place.

To provide access to the loft, install a vertical ladder with round rungs (page 118, center) or an angled ship's ladder with treads supported by wooden cleats or dadoes. For greater comfort and convenience, you can put in a prefabricated wooden stairway or iron spiral stairway. A low protective railing around a sleeping platform is usually fairly lightweight and need be no more than 24 inches high; railing for a large deck should be a minimum of 36 inches above the deck and must be sturdy enough to bear the full weight of an adult. If you need storage space under a loft, you may want to build standard 2-by-4 stud walls be-

neath it as frames for closet partitions.

Keep the loft sparse and simple. Carpeting is the most common floor covering, favored for its sound-absorbing capacity. In a loft with restricted headroom, use subdued or indirect lighting: standard lamps and ceiling fixtures can create unwanted heat and glare in the confined space. And because a loft is generally the warmest area in the room, build your loft in an area that has good cross-ventilation from nearby windows.

A simple platform. This sleeping loft, set 4 feet beneath the ceiling, has an outer end supported by heavy posts and an inner end secured to the wall studs. The frame consists of standard construction-grade lumber, except for decorative facing boards of clear wood fastened to exposed frame edges; the flooring consists of plywood panels. A dowel ladder provides easy access, and the railing balusters are spaced closely enough to protect a small child from danger.

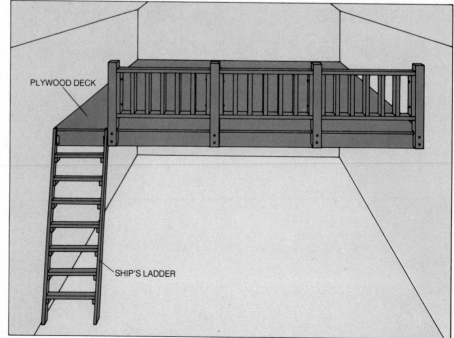

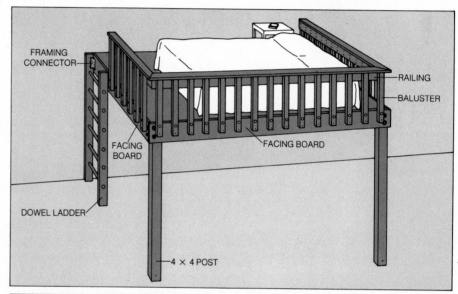

A large-scale loft. This so-called bridge loft spans the space between two bearing walls. Its plywood floor is supported by full-scale joists, which in turn hang on ledgers lag-bolted into the wall studs. A cathedral ceiling allows ample headroom for standing, and an angled ship's ladder permits easy access to the loft yet takes up little space in the room below. For lofts as big as this one, most building codes require a strong railing at least waist-high.

Building a Sleeping Loft

1 **Installing the ledger.** Using a chalk line and a level, mark the wall for the bottom of the loft platform; below this line, mark the positions of the wall-stud centers. Cut a 2-by-4 ledger to the length of the platform, set it against the wall with its top edge at the marked line and each end about halfway between a pair of studs, and tack the ledger temporarily in place. Drill pilot holes through the ledger and the studs for ⅜-inch lag bolts 4 inches long, and fasten the ledger to the studs with lag bolts and washers.

In a masonry wall, drive bolts into lead shields embedded in the masonry at 24-inch intervals.

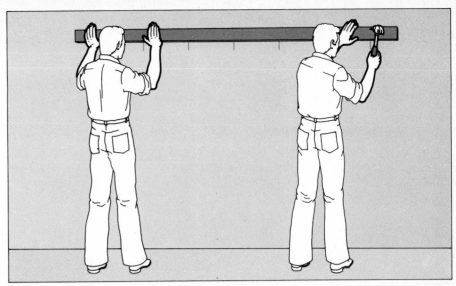

2 **Assembling the platform frame.** Working on the floor, build a rectangular framework of joists nailed between two header joists—in this example all the joists are 2-by-6s. Mark the headers for joist centers 16 inches apart and face-nail each end of a joist in place with three 16-penny nails driven through a header joist; use a combination square to check for right angles.

3 **Completing the frame.** Nail 2-by-4 blocking between the tops of joists at the points where the edges of ½-inch plywood subflooring will meet. Working over the area of one panel at a time, spread construction adhesive in a wavy pattern on the tops of the joists and blocking, then secure each panel with the face grain perpendicular to the joists, using eightpenny resin-coated nails at 6-inch intervals.

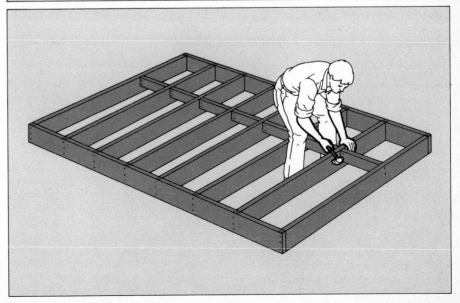

4 **Attaching facing boards.** Cut three ¾-inch boards, long enough to fit around the three exposed sides of the platform and wide enough to cover the joist sides and the edges of the plywood—1-by-8s if you use 2-by-6 joists. Turn the platform bottom side up. Nail the boards to the joists, their tops flush with the top of the plywood, by driving three eightpenny finishing nails at the ends and additional nails every 16 inches in a staggered pattern.

5 **Raising the platform.** Cut two 4-by-4 posts to the height of the bottom of the plywood deck above the floor and, with helpers, lift the platform into place. Rest the rear header joist on the ledger and, while one helper holds this header against the wall, set the 4-by-4 posts within the forward corners formed by the front header and the end joists. Above each of the ledger's lag bolts, drill pilot holes through the rear header and into the studs and fasten the header to the studs with lag bolts and washers the same size as those you used on the ledger.

6 **Bolting the posts in place.** While your helpers steady the posts, use a level to check that the platform is level both parallel and perpendicular to the wall, then have the helpers mark the posts at the bottoms of the joists. If a post is too long, trim it. If one is too short, drive shims between the top of the post and the plywood deck (*inset*). When the shims hold the platform at the marks on the posts, drive a nail through the deck and shims into the tops of the posts.

With the post marks aligned with the bottoms of the joists, drill holes through the joists and posts for two ¼-inch carriage bolts at the front and two at the sides of each corner, staggering the holes so the bolts do not intersect.

7 **Securing the posts to the floor.** Check that the front and sides of each post are plumb and mark the floor at the post bottoms for reference; then toenail each post to the floor with two tenpenny nails driven from opposite sides.

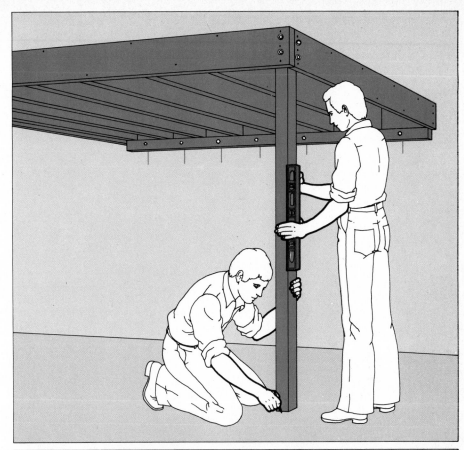

8 **Setting balusters for a railing.** Tack balusters—30-inch 2-by-2s—to the facing boards of the platform, overlapping the facing board by 6 inches. Space balusters 5 inches apart but leave an opening at least 26 inches wide for the entrance to the loft.

Plumb each baluster with a level, drill a hole for a ¼-inch carriage bolt 3 inches below the platform floor, and bolt the baluster in place.

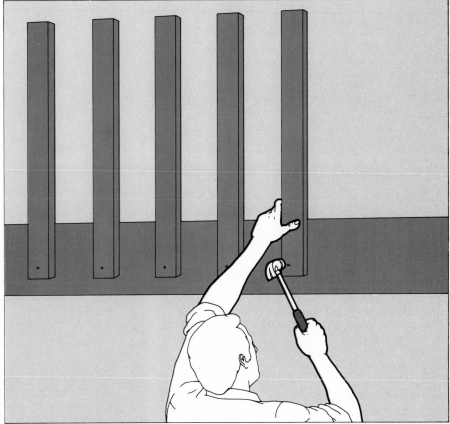

9 **Topping the railing.** Hold a 1-by-6 flat along the inside of each row of balusters, flush with the baluster tops, and screw the boards in place. Attach 1-by-4 boards—cut at the corners for miter or butt joints—flat on top of the balusters with one edge flush with the inner faces of the 1-by-6s *(inset)*, and nail these topping boards to the balusters and to the 1-by-6s.

Building a Bridge Loft

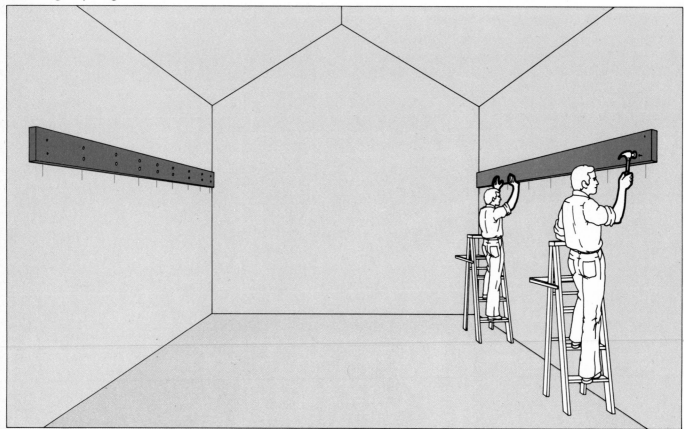

1 **Installing the ledgers.** Mark the positions of ledgers and studs on opposite walls *(page 113, Step 1)* and cut the ledgers—in this example, 2-by-10s—so that each one reaches from a corner to a point 5 inches beyond the outermost stud. With a helper, nail each ledger to a stud near the corner and to the outermost stud, using two 16-penny nails at each stud.

Drill two pilot holes through the ledgers and into each intermediate stud for ⅜-inch lag bolts 5 inches long, and fasten the ledgers in place.

2 **Installing the joists.** At 16-inch intervals, nail joist hangers to the ledgers, with the bottoms of the hangers flush with the bottoms of the ledgers; then, with a helper, fit the joists in place—if a joist has a bow, set the bow upward—and nail the joists to the hangers.

3 **Laying down the floor.** Cut blocking pieces from joist stock and nail them between joists where the edges of plywood panels will meet; then run construction adhesive over the joists and the blocking and install panels of ¾-inch plywood (*page 113, Step 3*). If you plan to cover the

loft with carpeting, extend the plywood flooring 1½ inches beyond the front joist. When you install a facing board (*Step 4, below*) directly below the plywood flooring, the part of the overhang that projects over the board will form a ¾-inch lip to shape and secure the edge of the carpet.

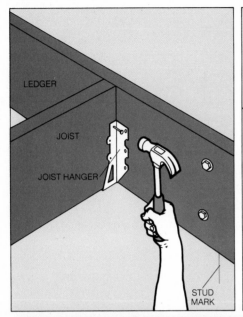

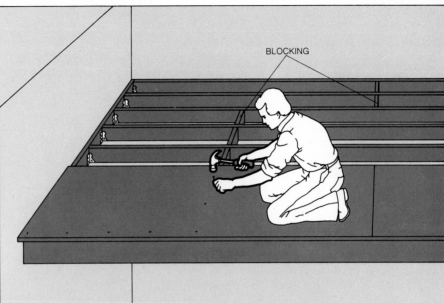

4 **Putting up a wallboard ceiling.** Make a T brace of 2-by-4s to the height of a ceiling under the loft. Apply adhesive to the bottoms of joists and to the blocking over the area of one wallboard panel at a time and, while a helper supports each

panel with the brace, nail it in place with 1⅜-inch wallboard nails. Finish the ceiling with wallboard tape and joint compound. Nail a facing board across the front of the loft. For an uncarpeted loft, set the top of the facing board flush

with the top of the plywood floor, as you would in a sleeping platform (*page 114, Step 4*). If you are planning to carpet the floor of the loft, set the top of the facing board directly against the underside of the plywood overhang.

5 **Building a railing.** Cut 54-inch posts from 4-by-4s, make a notch 1 inch deep and 10 inches long at one end of each post and, at 4-foot intervals, lag-bolt the posts to the loft frame, with the notches against the facing boards; if the loft has a plywood overhang for carpeting, notch the plywood to receive the posts. Build rectangular frames of 2-by-4s, each 35 by 48 inches, and fill the frames with 2-by-4 balusters spaced 5 inches apart. With a helper, set a frame between each pair of posts, with the top of the frame 4 inches below the tops of the posts, and attach each frame side to a post with two lag bolts. Leave a space open for a loft entrance.

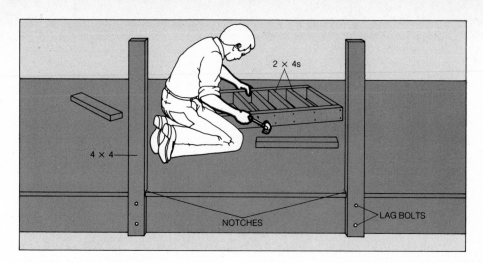

A Simple Ladder

Assembling the parts. Cut two 2-by-4 stringers to the height of the deck and drill 1⅝-inch holes through their faces at equal intervals no more than 1 foot apart; cut standard 1⅝-inch wood closet rod into 26-inch lengths, glue them into the holes with the end grain vertical and drive fourpenny finishing nails through the backs of the stringers and into the dowels.

Secure the top of the ladder to the platform with right-angle framing connectors and toenail the bottom to the floor.

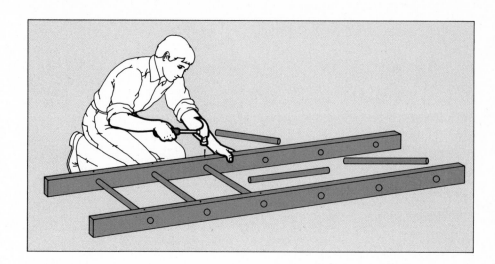

A Staircase Ladder

1 **Marking the stringers.** After notching a plywood overhang for a 27-inch opening, set a 2-by-6 stringer against the platform deck at the angle of the ladder—typically about 60°—and, using a level, mark the bottom of the stringer with a horizontal line and the top with a vertical line directly upward from the edge of the platform. Cut the board at both lines and use it as a template to cut a second stringer.

2 **Installing the cleats.** To determine the number of treads, divide the vertical distance between the deck and floor by 12 and round off the result to the nearest whole number; to determine the spacing between treads, divide the same vertical distance by the number of treads. Tack a stringer to the platform and use a level to mark horizontal cleat lines directly below the level of each tread. Take the stringer down and duplicate the lines on the second stringer. For the cleats, cut 5½-inch lengths of 1-by-3 and screw them in place between the stringers, with their tops flush with the lines and their front edges flush with the fronts of the stringers, using four 2-inch No. 8 screws for each cleat.

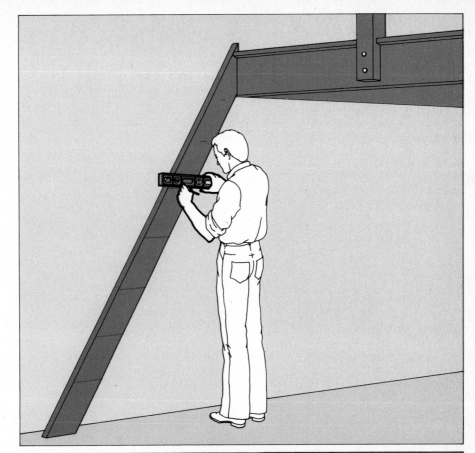

3 **Completing the ladder.** Cut 2-foot 2-by-6 treads, set them on the cleats and secure them with eightpenny box nails driven through the stringers and into the end grain of the treads. Raise the ladder into position and secure the stringers at the top with framing connectors and at the bottom by toenailing. Saw off any projecting triangles at the tops of the stringers, above the platform deck.

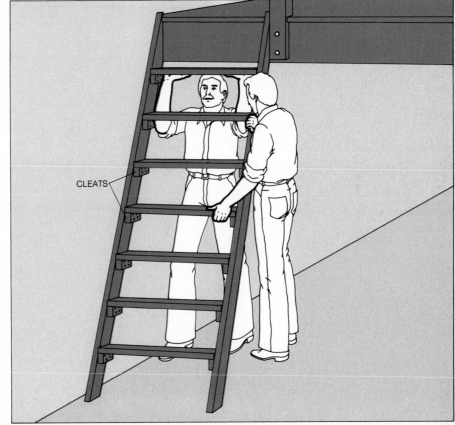

CLEATS

4

New Life for Old Built-ins

A new bottom for a dovetailed drawer. The broken bottom of this drawer cannot be removed easily. It fits into dadoes in the sides of the drawer, and the drawer back, which also holds the bottom in place, is fitted to the sides with intricate dovetail joints. As the first step in a repair, the bottom must be cut into pieces and removed; a new bottom is simply installed with cleats and the thin wire nails called brads.

Most houses come with built-ins, and in time these built-ins break, wear out or fail to meet new needs. But you need not take on the labor and cost of making new ones if you can repair and remodel the old. Renovating the furniture shown in Chapter 2 or the platforms of Chapter 3 is a straightforward job—the parts fit together as they would in a piece built from scratch, and you need only replace them. Cabinets, however, with their drawers, doors and precise joinery, present special difficulties.

Many older cabinets, particularly those built before 1940, were put together by the carpenters who built the house—and such cabinets seldom follow the designs of modern cabinet specialists, whose techniques are illustrated in Chapter 1. As often as not, old cabinets were nailed to the walls piece by piece and held together by an assortment of butt joints, cleats and glue blocks; drawers and doors may have been added in a variety of unconventional ways, as the need for them arose. Even some newer, shop-built cabinets are made of materials difficult to work, such as particleboard and sheet metal, rather than high-quality plywood. Repairing either type of cabinet calls for ingenuity, resourcefulness and the skills of an oldtime carpenter—or perhaps of an auto-body repairman.

Some old cabinets can be renovated with conventional woodworking tricks—worn screwholes are tightened with matchsticks and glue, doors are planed to fit, loose glue joints refastened. But often these expedients are inadequate. For one thing, they cannot remedy faults in the original construction of the cabinet—shelves made too long and now visibly sagging, or a badly constructed door that has warped. A damaged part—a scorched section of countertop, for example—may be impossible to replace invisibly. The solutions to such problems are not subtle: the shelf must be propped up with an extra partition, the door pulled straight with a stiff oak strip, the scorched section routed out or cut away entirely and replaced with a contrasting material. Such fixes should not be hidden; indeed, they may look worse if you attempt to conceal them. The only way to keep them from becoming eyesores is to do a neat, workmanlike job and let the repair speak for itself.

With very old cabinets, the major problem may be the design itself. Kitchen cabinets with tilting flour bins, tin-lined bread compartments, odd-sized drawers and no partitions or floor at all make no provision for modern cookware and appliances. Many old bookcases have shelves too shallow for stereo gear and too closely spaced for large books. The only solution is to gut the cabinet interior and remodel it—substituting drawers for shelves (or vice versa), for example, or adding space-saving features of modern cabinets.

Why Cabinets Break—and How to Fix Them

Sooner or later, the strains of age and use will damage even the sturdiest built-in. For the furniture and platforms described in Chapters 2 and 3, repairs are relatively straightforward: a broken part is replaced or an entire piece is reassembled by the same method that was used to build it.

Cabinets, with their moving parts and special points of stress, are another matter. Doors warp; shelves sag; drawer bottoms crack; surfaces are burned, scratched or dented; and an entire cabinet frame may be forced out of plumb or twisted out of shape. These ills are like ailments of a body, calling for exact diagnoses and specific remedies.

The first step in diagnosis is to determine the type of cabinets you have. Most modern homes contain prefabricated cabinets like those in Chapter 1, with backs and with hanging strips for securing the cabinets to a wall. Older houses may have backless cabinets, built by nailing cleats to a wall, then nailing shelves, sides and a frame to the cleats. A prefabricated cabinet is generally repaired as a unit, a backless cabinet piece by piece.

Next, determine the problem. Sagging out of level is the most common, but cabinets can also rack—that is, twist out of square. You can best repair a sagging prefabricated cabinet by removing it from the wall and reinstalling it (below and opposite, Steps 1 and 2; pages 46-51). You may be able to repair a sagging backless cabinet by pushing it against the wall and renailing its parts into place. If the sag is caused by a settling or deformed wall, the cabinet must be taken apart and reassembled on the wall (opposite right, Steps 1 and 2).

To diagnose a racked cabinet that has twisted away from the wall, check the joints. If they are square and in good condition, insert shims between the cabinet and the wall to push the cabinet back into square (page 47, Step 2). Joints that have popped loose must be reglued, a remedy that calls for removing the cabinet from the wall.

Like the cabinets that hold them, shelves can sag from overloading. An adjustable shelf can simply be flipped over—a "repair" that can be repeated almost endlessly. Permanently fastened shelves should be permanently bolstered with support partitions (below, left).

A support for a sagging shelf. At an end of the cabinet or bookcase, measure the distance from the bottom of the sagging shelf to the top of the shelf below. Cut a ¾-inch board as deep as the shelf and as long as the measured distance and force this partition under the sag; then butt-nail it in place through the sagging shelf and toenail it to the shelf below.

If the lower shelf is also the bottom of the cabinet, it will support the partition permanently. If it is not, it will eventually sag below the partition; install additional partitions, working downward, until you reach the cabinet bottom.

Squaring a Racked Cabinet

1 **Straightening the cabinet.** Detach the cabinet from the wall by removing the screws in the hanging strip, then apply glue to any joints that have popped open—if the joints have not opened enough to admit glue, tap them open with a hammer and wood block. Close the joints with two bar clamps, set near the ends of the top and bottom rail. Check the squareness of the cabinet by measuring diagonally across opposite corners (page 27, Step 3); if the measurements are not equal, loosen the clamps, gently push one corner of the cabinet inward until the measurements are equal, then retighten the clamps.

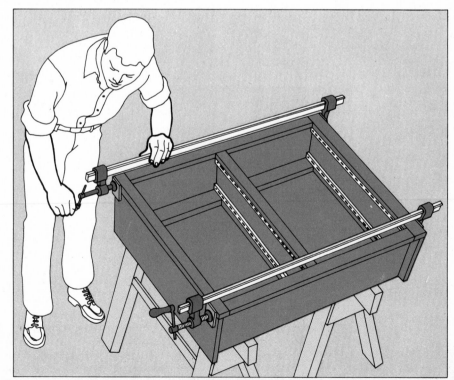

2 Strengthening the cabinet. An inch from the front and back of the cabinet, screw metal angle braces to the joints between the top and the sides. To strengthen the bottom joints, cut 1-by-1-inch blocks as long as the cabinet depth. At each joint, spread glue on two adjacent sides of a block, set the glued sides along the joint of the bottom and a side, and then fasten it with six 1¼-inch No. 4 screws, driving three screws into the bottom and three into the side.

Rehanging a Backless Cabinet

1 Taking the cabinet apart. Place a wood block against the inside of the front frame and tap it with a hammer completely around the frame to loosen the joints. Grip the frame and pull it away from the shelves and sides—the nails will come out with the frame. Remove the sides and shelves in the same way, but leave the cleats beneath the shelves (inset) on the wall.

2 Straightening the cleats. Use a cat's paw to remove some of the nails that fasten each sagging cleat to the wall studs, leaving the nail at the high end of a cleat in place. Push the sagging end of the cleat upward, using a level to check its position; when the cleat is level, trace its bottom edge on the wall for reference. Refasten the cleat with nails driven well below the existing nail holes, to be sure that the new nails will not slip into the old holes. Reassemble the cabinet in reverse order—first shelves, then sides and finally front frame.

Repairing the Moving Parts

When cabinet doors and drawers stick shut or will not close, check for small problems first. The trouble in a sticking drawer may be nothing more than a loose nail rubbing against a guide; hammer the nail back into place. A door may have a loose hinge, easily repaired by tightening the screws; if you find that the screws do not grip the wood of the door and front frame, plug the screw holes with wooden matchsticks driven into the holes and bound together with glue.

A major warp in a door may be visible to the eye; the correct remedy is a strong oak brace (right, bottom). If you suspect a minor warp in a sticking door or drawer but cannot see one, use a cabinetmaker's trick to make it visible. Run a piece of chalk along the suspected edge or guide, then close the door or drawer several times. The chalk will rub onto the cabinet and indicate the areas to be planed away.

A deformation of the frame is more serious. Check the cabinet in each direction with a level and by measuring the diagonals from corner to corner (page 27, Step 3). If the cabinet has sagged or is racked, you will probably have to remove and resquare it (pages 122-123).

Drawers are most likely to break down at certain points of special strain—bottoms, backstops and guides. Do not attempt to repair a bottom that has cracked or warped: It is best to remove the back of the drawer and slide a new bottom into the dadoes of the drawer sides. If the dadoes themselves are also damaged, install a set of cleats over the dadoes for the new bottom to rest upon.

After thousands of bumps from the back of a closing drawer, backstops are eventually pushed out of place or dislodged completely: Replace or thicken them with pieces of new wood. Wooden guides at the bottom of a drawer can be replaced with modern metal hardware; along the sides you must duplicate the old guides, because the metal type needs more room at the sides of a drawer than the cabinet provides.

After repairing or replacing any moving part of a cabinet, prolong its life by rubbing paraffin on every edge or surface that slides upon another.

Two Ways to Fix a Deformed Drawer

Planing an edge. Remove the door from the cabinet and, on the inner side, mark a line ⅛ inch from the edge that rubs or from high spots that have been marked by chalk; secure the door in a vise. On a lipped door, as in this example, use a rabbet plane or block plane to bevel the inside edge down to the marked line. On a flush door, use a block plane, taking special care not to plane the part of the bevel near the outside edge—if you shave any wood from that edge, you will widen the critical gap between the closed door and the front frame of the cabinet.

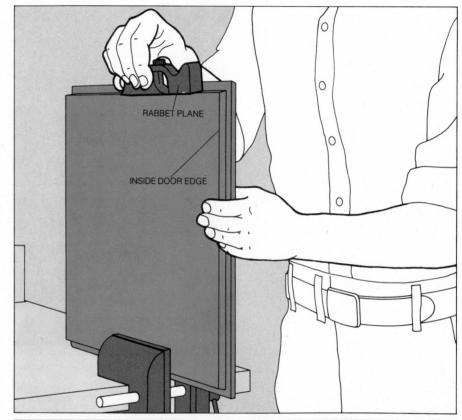

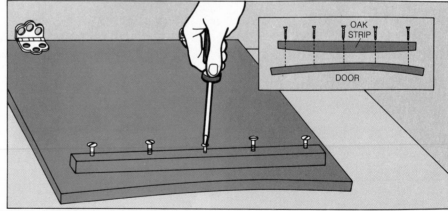

Bracing a warped door. Cut a strip of oak 2 inches shorter than the warped edge of the door, set the door face down and center the strip an inch in from the warped edge. At 6-inch intervals, drive and countersink 1½-inch No. 6 screws through the strip into the door. If you have removed the warp, unfasten the strip, glue it in place and refasten it.

If the strip does not work, remove it and use a block plane to give it a curve opposite of the curve of the warp. Reattach the strip with the opposite curves facing each other (inset). If necessary, deepen the curve of the strip repeatedly until the warp is eliminated. For a severe warp, soak the door a few hours and tighten the screws gradually so you do not crack the door.

Simple Cures for Ailing Drawers

Supporting a new bottom. If the sides of a drawer are cracked or if you cannot easily remove the drawer back to slide in a new bottom (in this example, dovetail joints make the back exceptionally difficult to remove), use cleats to support a new bottom dropped in from above. Cut two cleats about ½ inch wide, ½ inch thick and as long as each drawer side and screw them to the sides, with the tops of the cleats just above the dado tops. Apply glue to the cleat tops and use a tack hammer and brads to fasten a ¼-inch plywood bottom to the cleats.

New stops on flush drawers. Remove the worn or damaged stop blocks, push the drawer in as far as it will go and measure the distance from the cabinet front to the drawer front. Cut two blocks, 1 inch square and slightly thinner than the measured distance, and tape them to the back of the drawer. Test the drawer in its opening and, if necessary, insert cardboard shims between the drawer back and the wood blocks until the drawer front fits flush with the cabinet front, then fasten the stops and shims permanently with glue and wire brads.

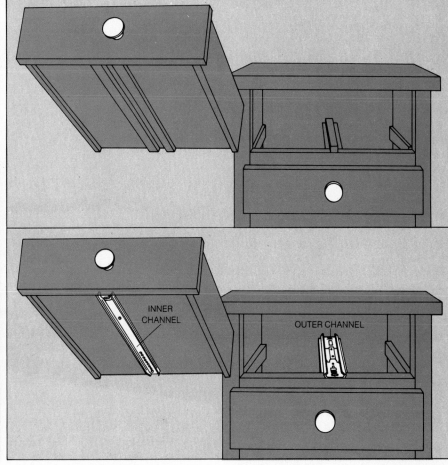

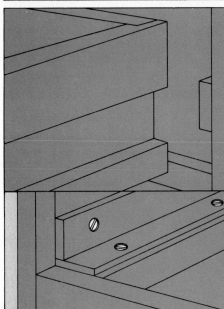

Replacing wooden side guides. In the top guide, a drawer side is dadoed to fit a cleat on a cabinet side or partition; in the bottom one, two cleats form a guide for a drawer to slide in. To replace guides, trace their outlines and remove them. Cut duplicate pieces and glue and screw them at the traced positions.

Replacing wooden bottom guides. A wooden center cleat, like the one at top, can be replaced by a homemade duplicate, but most professional repairmen prefer metal center guides, which come in sizes to fit most drawers. Remove the wooden guides, measure the drawer depth and buy a center guide to match it.

Draw a center line down the drawer bottom and the drawer support below, if there is one—the guides will work with or without a support. Fit the inner channel to the drawer bottom and the outer channel to the cabinet, then test the drawer in its opening—if it is too low, insert cardboard shims below the outer channel.

Getting Rid of Stains, Nicks and Dents

In a wooden surface such as butcher block, small dents and nicks may be acceptable or even welcome—they give the wood a certain character. In plastic laminate countertops or metal cabinets, they are eyesores to be eliminated. For plastic-laminate countertops, fillers in a variety of colors are commercially available; for metal cabinets, use touch-up paint.

In any material, large areas of damage call for more drastic measures. Butcher block must be scraped down or sanded. In plastic laminate, sections as large as 16 by 21 inches can be replaced with an inset of another material, such as ceramic tile, butcher block, or a ceramic-glass chopping board. In metal cabinets, large dents must be leveled and filled.

Insets for plastic laminates are installed by two different methods: butcher-block and ceramic-glass cutting boards are generally set in a hole in the countertop and supported by a metal rim, much like that of a sink; tiles can be cemented to a plywood base set into a routed-out area. The hole for the first method should not be cut through bracing or partitions; with the second method, make sure the insert material is not too heavy for the thinned portion of the countertop.

The remedy for a large dent in metal depends on its depth. A dent deeper than ½ inch must be popped out from inside the cabinet to a depth of ½ inch or less, then leveled with the type of filler used for automobile-body work; for a dent no deeper than ½ inch, use the filler directly. Sand, clean and spray-paint a leveled dent to restore the finish, working outdoors or in a well-ventilated area.

Replacing a Section of Plastic Laminate

1 **Cutting the hole.** Using the rim or a template provided by its manufacturer, mark the countertop. Just inside the corner, drill a hole for a saber-saw blade, then cut three sides of the opening. Along the cut, drive a few nails at a 45° angle into the edge of the waste piece (*inset*), to keep it from falling and splintering the countertop as the cut is completed. Finish the cut, reach under the countertop to support the waste piece and have a helper pull the nails.

Test-fit the metal rim in the opening and, if necessary, use a file to remove excess material.

COUNTERTOP

WASTE PIECE

INSIDE FLANGE

TABS

OUTSIDE FLANGE

2 **Preparing the insert.** Set the rim upside down and squeeze a thin bead of silicone-type caulking along its inside flange; then fit the inset piece—turned upside down—into the rim and use a screwdriver to push the metal tabs along the rim over the surface of the piece. Apply a heavier bead of caulking to the outside flange of the rim, then set the assembly into the countertop.

3 Fastening the inset. Working below the countertop, fit the hook of one of the lugs provided by the manufacturer over the edge of the metal rim, insert the lug bolt and thread it into an anchor pad, then screw the pad against the underside of the inset piece. For a rim 16 by 21 inches, position two lugs at each end, three on each side. Tighten opposite bolts sequentially, as you would the wheel lugs of an automobile, turning them just tight enough so that you cannot turn them with your fingers. On the countertop, use a spatula or putty knife to remove excess caulking at the edges of the inset and the rim.

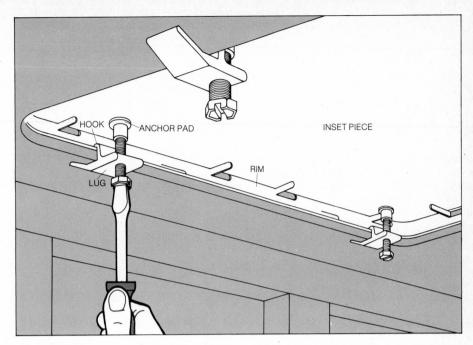

Installing an Inset of Tiles

1 Starting the router. Make an open, four-sided plywood jig to the insert dimensions plus the distance between the bit and base of your router and clamp the jig to the countertop. Set the router bit to half the depth of the tile plus the plywood base, tilt the router base to raise the bit above the countertop and set the base against an interior side of the jig. Turn on the router and slowly lower the bit into the countertop.

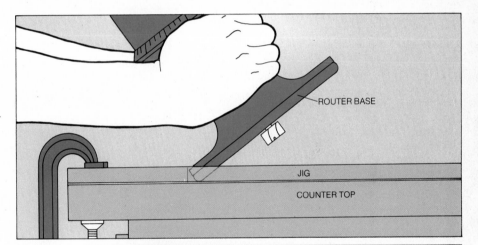

2 Routing the inset area. Move the router to the center of the inset area. Working clockwise, rout out increasingly large concentric circles until the router base touches the jig, then follow the edges of the jig completely around the inset area. Repeat the process with the bit set at the full depth of the base and tiles.

To square the corners, use a smaller router bit. At each corner, shift the jig outward, and use the small bit to carve corners that match your tiles.

3 **Laying the tiles.** Glue a rectangle of ¼-inch plywood to the routed area and cover it with tile mastic, then set the tiles on the mastic and let the mastic harden for 24 hours. Fill all the joints in the tiled area with grout or silicone caulking.

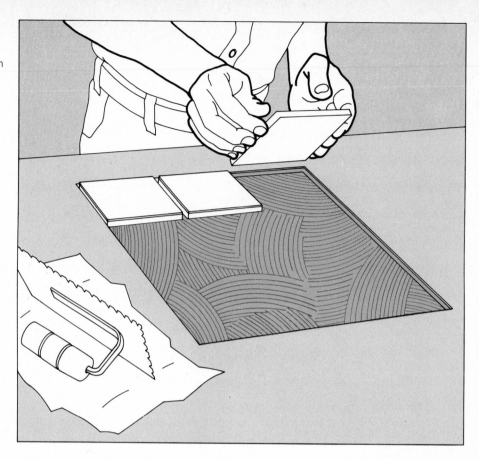

Restoring a Blemished Butcher Block

Scraping the damage. Set the edge of a refinishing scraper, available in hardware stores, against the butcher block at an angle of about 60° and, applying even pressure, pull the scraper over the blemished area. If, after about ten strokes, the blemish is not removed by the scraper, run a belt sander over the area—be careful not to hold the sander in one spot long enough to make a depression in the surface.

Filling a Dent in Metal

1 Applying the filler. Using coarse sandpaper, rub off the paint in the dented area and roughen a 1-inch rim around its border, then press plastic body filler, available at auto-supply stores, into the dent with the applicator provided by the manufacturer. Apply enough filler to raise the area slightly above the surrounding surface—the filler will shrink as it dries.

Using coarse sandpaper wrapped around a wood block, level the hardened filler flush with the surface, then smooth it with fine sandpaper. Wipe off any dust and paint flecks with a cloth soaked in rubbing alcohol.

2 Painting the surface. Cut a hole the size of the damaged area in a piece of cardboard. Hold this template 8 inches from the dent, hold a can of aerosol primer 10 inches from the template, and mist on a thin coat of primer, directing the spray from side to side. Let the primer dry.

Roughen the primer surface with fine wet-and-dry silicon-carbide sandpaper dipped in slightly soapy water—the soap will ease the job and clean the surface. Wipe the sanded surface with an alcohol-soaked cloth. Follow the procedure used to apply the primer and apply a coat of aerosol finish paint through the template. When the paint has dried, wet-sand and clean the surface, and spray on a second coat of paint. Finally, buff the surface with a soft, clean cloth.

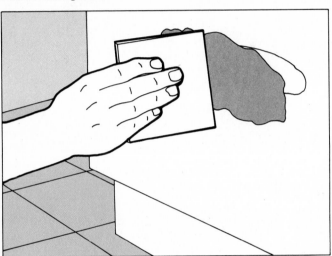

Popping a Deep Dent

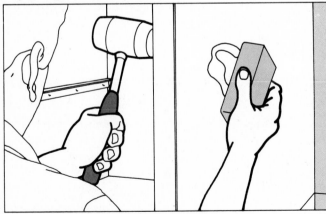

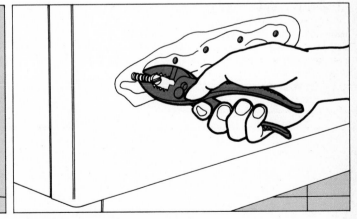

Pounding out the dent. If you can reach behind the dented area, hold a 2-by-4 or 4-by-4 block over the outside of the dented area and pound out the dent from inside with a plastic-faced mallet. If you cannot remove the dent this way, pound it out to a depth of ½ inch or less, then follow the procedure in Step 1, above, left.

For a narrow dent, use a flat metal plate rather than a wood block, and a metal hammer.

Pulling out the dents. If you cannot reach inside the dented area, drill holes through it at 2-inch intervals. Thread a self-tapping sheet-metal screw into an end hole, grip the screwhead with pliers (preferably locking-grip pliers) and pull the screw out until the surrounding part of the dent is no more than ½ inch deep. Repeat the procedure in each hole to the middle of the area, then start at the opposite end and work back to the middle. Proceed to Step 1, above, left.

Reorganizing Inside Space for Efficiency

A built-in cabinet with a door and deep shelves makes a poor container for small, flat objects, and a cabinet with drawers is unsuitable for storing china. But if your cabinets do not match your present needs, you need not build new units; with simple carpentry and inexpensive hardware, you can substitute shelves for drawers in one cabinet (installing a partition and a bottom, if necessary), or switch from a door to drawers in another.

With even less work and trouble, you can increase the number of shelves in a unit by mounting new shelves on the back of a door, or add work space with a large cutting board that slides beneath the countertop. Or you can modify existing fittings with such improvements as slide-out shelves or vertical partitions, which are handy for storing large cooking and serving pieces.

Before you can fashion most interior improvements, you will have to gut the cabinet. The job may be simple: To clear away doors, drawers on metal glides or shelves on metal brackets, you need only unscrew the supporting hardware. Wood mountings in old cabinets are harder to dismantle: some can be unscrewed, but most are bonded in place by old, tough animal glues. The mountings must be sawed into pieces, then knocked away from the cabinet walls or partitions with a hammer. Remaining nailheads must be cut off and rough places filled with wood putty. A keyhole saw is handy for cutting inside the confined reaches of an old cabinet. Stop sawing if the blade hits a nail or screw; either start a new cut or finish the cut with a hacksaw.

After you clear away the interior mountings, inspect the cabinet carefully. Repair loose joints and sagging or racked units by the methods described on pages 122-123. If you plan to increase the load in a wall cabinet, reinforce its mountings with extra screws; add a hinge to a door on which you will hang shelves.

Switching from Drawers to Shelves

1 **Gutting the interior.** Remove the drawers, then cut the rails from the front frame of the cabinet as close to the sides of the openings as the fittings inside the cabinet will allow. If wooden drawer guides and supports are secured to the front and back of the cabinet, as in this example, saw them in half with a keyhole saw and break out the pieces with a hammer. To remove guides and supports that are screwed and glued to the side walls, extract the screws and tap the wood with a hammer to break the glue bonds. Cut off any remaining nails or screws with a hacksaw or nippers. Finally, cut the stub ends of the drawer rails back flush with the edges of the opening. Cover the cut edges with wood putty, let the putty dry and sand the surface smooth.

2 **Fastening cleats for a partition.** Inside a cabinet that does not have a central partition, fasten vertical 1-by-1 cleats to the front and back with screws and glue. To locate the back cleat, use a combination square to align a straight board square with the front of the cabinet at the top and bottom corners of the opening *(inset)*. Mark points on the back wall directly opposite the corners. Draw a vertical line ½ inch from these marks beyond the door opening. Secure the cleat along the line; similarly mount the front cleat ½ inch away from the opening.

Cut a partition from ½-inch plywood for a snug fit between the front and back walls of the cabinet and tall enough to extend from the underside of the counter to the floor.

GUIDE
SUPPORT
RAIL STUB

3 **Installing the partition.** In the partition, start three finishing nails, spaced evenly on a line ⅜ inch from the front and back edges; spread glue on the cleats, then hold the partition against them and nail it in place. If the partition will not fit through the opening, saw it in two horizontally and mount the halves separately.

4 **Putting in a bottom.** Glue and screw a horizontal 1-by-1 cleat to the cabinet front, with its top edge ½ inch below the door opening. Use a level to draw lines on the side wall and partition at the same height as the front cleat and secure cleats along this line. Cut a bottom from ½-inch plywood, apply glue to the top of each cleat and lay the bottom shelf on the cleats. Nail the shelf to the cleats. Finally, fit the cabinet with a door (*pages 37-40*) and install adjustable shelves (*page 10*) or other dividers.

Switching from Shelves to Drawers

1 **Clearing the space.** To remove shelves glued into dadoes, use a saber saw to start a V that converges at the back of the shelf, and use a keyhole saw to finish the cut; if the shelf extends through more than one section of the cabinet, make V cuts in each section, then saw lengthwise along the middle of the shelf to connect the Vs. Tap the top and bottom of the remaining shelf pieces with a hammer to loosen the glue, then gently work them free. If you have cut shelves that run through more than one section, install a partition between the sections (*page 131*).

To remove a shelf mounted on cleats, tap the shelf from below to break the glue bond and pry it off. Unscrew the cleats, tap them to break the glue bond and remove them. Use a hacksaw to cut off any protruding nail or screw tips.

Cut and install wood spacers for drawer glides in each drawer opening (*page 36, Step 1*).

2 **Toenailing drawer rails.** Cut rails of ¾-inch plywood to fit snugly between the drawers—use a paint scraper to clean varnish or paint from the edges of the opening where the rails will fit—and start nails at a 45° angle on the top and bottom of each rail, ½ inch from each end, driving the nails until their tips just emerge from the ends *(inset)*. Apply glue to the ends of each rail, fit it in place and drive the nails, wedging a length of scrap wood under the rail to brace it as you drive the upper nail. Use a nail set to countersink the nailheads. Mount and adjust the drawer glides *(page 36, Steps 2 and 3)*.

Built-in Conveniences for a Built-in Cabinet

An extra working top. This pull-out cutting board is mounted between two sets of 1-by-1 hardwood runs, cut like cleats and spaced ¹/₁₆ inch wider than the thickness of the board. To begin its assembly, screw the runs to a side wall and a partition. Install a rail under the cutting board and screw a stop block to the underside of the board, 6 inches from its back. Screw a pull-out knob to the front edge. Wipe the board periodically with mineral oil to help it move freely in its runs and to keep it water-resistant.

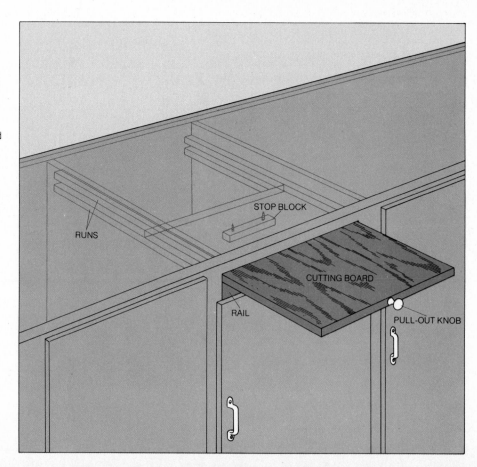

RUNS

STOP BLOCK

CUTTING BOARD

RAIL

PULL-OUT KNOB

A set of door shelves. Build the sides and shelves of this door-back unit with ½-inch plywood; use ¼-inch plywood for the back and for the edge bands, which keep objects from sliding or toppling off the shelves when the door swings. A 4-inch shelf is wide enough to hold most cans, but in planning the unit, to make sure that the shelf assembly will not block the swing of the door, tape a full-sized cardboard model of the bottom shelf to the back of the door and then close the door. Mount the unit on the door with four screws and countersink washers; add an extra hinge to the door to support the added weight of the shelves.

If necessary, as in this example, cut back the existing shelf or shelves inside the cabinet with a saber saw so that there will be room for the new shelves when the door is closed.

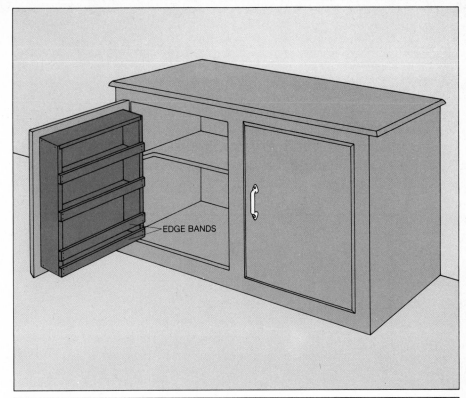

EDGE BANDS

Easy access to corners. These identical quarter-round shelf units swing out for easy access when the cabinet door is opened, but rest neatly inside the cabinet when the door is closed (*inset*). The sides and shelves are made of ½-inch plywood, the edge bands are of ¼-inch plywood, and the shelf radius is 2 inches less than the width of the door opening. Attach one unit to the back of the door with screws and countersink washers. Mount the other on the edge of the cabinet stile, using two 3-inch butt hinges; the hinge pins should extend past the edge of the stile to allow a 180° swing.

If the door hinges are on the side nearer the corner, rehang the door to reverse its swing.

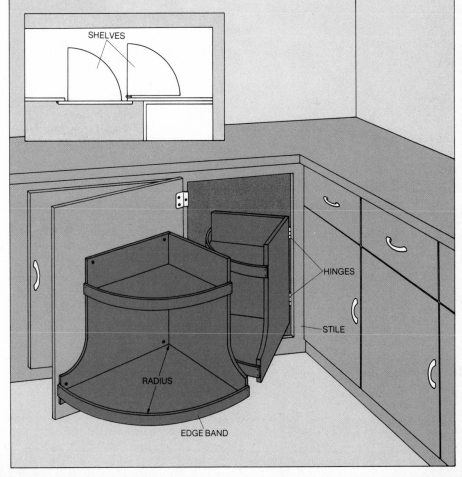

SHELVES

HINGES

STILE

RADIUS

EDGE BAND

Picture Credits

The sources for the illustrations in this book are shown below. The drawings are by Jack Arthur, Roger C. Essley, Fred Holz, Dick Lee, Joan McGurren and Bill McWilliams. Credits for the pictures from left to right are separated by semicolons, from top to bottom by dashes.

Cover: Fil Hunter. 6: Stephen R. Brown. 8-15: John Massey. 16-21: Ray Skibinski. 22-25: Gerry Gallagher. 26-41: Walter Hilmers Jr. 44-55: Frederic F. Bigio from B-C Graphics. 56-60: Ray Skibinski. 61-64: Eduino Pereira. 65: Robert Perron, Gamal El-Zoghby, architect. 66: Robert Perron, The Hillier Group, architects—Norman McGrath, William Ehrlich, designer. 67: Michael Boys from Susan Griggs Agency, London, Piero Castellini, designer—Carla de Benedetti, Milan, Carla Venosta, designer. 68: Aldo Ballo, Milan, Adriano Campioni, architect—Emmett Bright, Rome, Giullo Coltelacci, designer. 69: Alfredo Anghinelli, Milan, Ascarelli, Macciocchi, Nicolao and Parisio, architects. 70: Robert Perron, Robert Nevins, architect—Carla de Benedetti, Milan, Lino Schenal, architect. 71: Michael Dunne, London, L. Durham and L. Weingarden, architects and designers, mural by Stan Peskett. 72: Stephen R. Brown. 74-79: Eduino Pereira. 80-89: Frederic F. Bigio from B-C Graphics. 90-95: John Massey. 96-101: Frederic F. Bigio from B-C Graphics. 102: Stephen R. Brown. 104-111: John Massey. 112-119: Walter Hilmers Jr. 120: Stephen R. Brown. 122-129: Whitman Studio, Inc. 130-133: Frederic F. Bigio from B-C Graphics.

Acknowledgments

The index/glossary for this book was prepared by Louise Hedberg. The editors also wish to thank the following: American Foam Centers, Arlington, Virginia; American Plywood Association, Tacoma, Washington; Bally Block Company, Bally, Pennsylvania; Chuck Barton, Damascus, Maryland; David Beach, Creative Space, Inc., Fairfax, Virginia; Richard W. Beatty, Alexandria, Virginia; Richard Benswanger, The Kitchen Shoppe, Alexandria, Virginia; A. E. Boland, Alexandria, Virginia; Richard Bue, Sico Incorporated, Minneapolis, Minnesota; Kevin Connors, Wood You, Inc., Washington, D.C.; R. J. De Cristoforo, Los Altos Hills, California; Horace Gifford, Designer, New York City; Hudee Manufacturing, Dallas, Texas; Michael E. Hughes, Alexandria, Virginia; Claude Lawrence, Alexandria, Virginia; Bill McPherson, Upper Marlboro, Maryland; Murphy Door Bed Company, New York City; National Paint and Coatings Association, Washington, D.C.; Larry Schultz, Carpentry Unlimited, Falls Church, Virginia; Larry Spitalny, Washington, D.C.; Vincent Vitale, New York City. The following persons also assisted in the writing of this book: James McNatt and Wendy Murphy.

Index/Glossary